ROUTLEDGE LIBRARY EDITIONS:
ETHICS

Volume 40

MORAL RELATIVISM AND REASONS FOR ACTION

MORAL RELATIVISM AND REASONS FOR ACTION

ROBERT STREIFFER

Routledge
Taylor & Francis Group

LONDON AND NEW YORK

First published in 2003 by Routledge

This edition first published in 2021
by Routledge
2 Park Square, Milton Park, Abingdon, Oxon OX14 4RN

and by Routledge
52 Vanderbilt Avenue, New York, NY 10017

Routledge is an imprint of the Taylor & Francis Group, an informa business

© 2003 Robert Streiffer

All rights reserved. No part of this book may be reprinted or reproduced or utilised in any form or by any electronic, mechanical, or other means, now known or hereafter invented, including photocopying and recording, or in any information storage or retrieval system, without permission in writing from the publishers.

Trademark notice: Product or corporate names may be trademarks or registered trademarks, and are used only for identification and explanation without intent to infringe.

British Library Cataloguing in Publication Data
A catalogue record for this book is available from the British Library

ISBN: 978-0-367-85624-3 (Set)
ISBN: 978-1-00-305260-9 (Set) (ebk)
ISBN: 978-0-367-51257-6 (Volume 40) (hbk)
ISBN: 978-1-00-305306-4 (Volume 40) (ebk)

Publisher's Note
The publisher has gone to great lengths to ensure the quality of this reprint but points out that some imperfections in the original copies may be apparent.

Disclaimer
The publisher has made every effort to trace copyright holders and would welcome correspondence from those they have been unable to trace.

MORAL RELATIVISM AND REASONS FOR ACTION

Robert Streiffer

Routledge
New York & London

Published in 2003 by
Routledge
29 West 35th Street
New York, NY 10001
www.routldge-ny.com

Published in Great Britain by
Routledge
11 New Fetter Lane
London EC4P 4EE
www.routledge.co.uk

Routledge is an imprint of the Taylor & Francis Group.
Printed in the United States of America on acid-free paper.

Copyright © 2003 by Robert Streiffer.

All rights reserved. No part of this book may be reprinted or reproduced or utilized in any form or by any electronic, mechanical, or other means, now known or hereafter invented, including photocopying and recording, or in any information storage or retrieval system, without permission in writing from the publisher.

10 9 8 7 6 5 4 3 2 1

Library of Congress Cataloging-in-Publication Data
Streiffer, Robert.
   Moral relativism and reasons for action / by Robert Streiffer.
    p. cm. — (Studies in ethics)
   Includes bibliographical references and index
   ISBN 0-415-93852-X (alk. paper)
   1. Ethical relativism. I. Title. II. Series: Studies in ethics (New York, N.Y.).
171'.7—dc21
[B]   2002014884

To Catherine

Contents

PREFACE	ix
ACKNOWLEDGMENTS	xi
INTRODUCTION	xiii

CHAPTER 1
APPRAISER RELATIVISM AND THE RELIABILITY OF OUR LINGUISTIC
INTUITIONS   3

1. Appraiser Relativism Defined   3
2. The Alleged Explanation of the Intractability of Moral
   Disagreements   6
3. Some Counterintuitive Implications of Appraiser Relativism   7
4. The First Two Strategies for Explaining Away Our Linguistic
   Intuitions   13
5. A Test for Determining the Reliability of Our Linguistic
   Intuitions   17
6. The Third Strategy for Explaining Away Our Linguistic
   Intuitions   18
7. Appraiser Relativism, Explanation, and the Reliability of Our
   Linguistic Intuitions   22
8. Summary and Concluding Remarks   25

CHAPTER 2
AGENT RELATIVISM AND REASONS FOR ACTION 29

   1. The Practicality Argument for Agent Relativism 29
   2. Two Arguments for Moral Universalism 31
   3. A Defense of the Practicality Requirement 33
   4. The Desire Argument for Reasons Relativism 38
   5. The Narrow Desire Argument for Reasons Relativism 44
   6. Summary 51

CHAPTER 3
REASONS FOR ACTION AND THE WAYS OF BEING GOOD 53

   1. The Project 53
   2. The Ways of Being Good 55
   3. The Ways of Being Good and Moral Requirements 64
   4. The Ways of Being Good and Reasons for Action 66
   5. The Quick Argument for the Relevance of Morality 70
   6. Some Advantages of the Quick Argument for the Relevance of Morality 71
   7. The Moral Requirements Thesis 75
   8. Difficulties for the Revised Reasons for Action Thesis 78
   9. The Revised Argument for the Relevance of Morality 81
   10. Difficulties for the Revised Argument for the Relevance of Morality 83
   11. Summary and Concluding Remarks 88

AFTERWORD 91
   1. Test and Appraiser Relativism in Other Areas 91
   2. Defining Moral Relativism 93

ENDNOTES 101
BIBLIOGRAPHY 109
INDEX 115

Preface

This book is a revised and expanded version of my dissertation, which I completed for the Ph.D. program at the Massachusetts Institute of Technology in 1999. The MIT Philosophy Department offers its Ph.D. students what is called "The Three-Paper Option." This allows students to submit three publication-quality papers on related topics rather than a single, dissertation-length work. I chose the three-paper option, and thus, although there is overlap in the topics, each chapter in this book can be read independently of the others.

Acknowledgments

Because this work is a revised and expanded version of my dissertation, the first expression of thanks goes to my dissertation committee: Judith Jarvis Thomson (Chair), Joshua Cohen, and Ralph Wedgwood. All three gave me extensive support and feedback during the writing process and during my years at MIT. Those who are familiar with them and with their work will, I hope, see their influence. I only wish their influence could have been greater.

Of the three, I worked most closely with Judy, and I therefore owe her a special thanks. Her clarity and uncompromising rigor, and her deep respect for intuition and common-sense continue to serve as ideals for me in my philosophical writings. Her untiring commitment to the welfare of the graduate students—whether it is in her role as teacher, dissertation advisor, or placement officer—motivates me in my relationships with my own graduate students now at the University of Wisconsin-Madison.

I would also like to thank all of the other MIT graduate students, most of whom have given me useful comments on some part or other of this book, and all of whom contributed to a friendly and collegial atmosphere. Special thanks go to Ishani Maitra and Andrew Botterell for their very helpful comments on every chapter. Here at the University of Wisconsin-Madison, Dennis Stampe gave me useful comments on chapter 3. Both Dennis and Dan Hausman provided constructive discussion on some of the issues raised in the Afterword. And thanks to both Sharon Van Sluijs and Sara Gavrell

Ortiz for their editorial comments on the entire work, and to Sara for her help on the index.

I would also like to extend my thanks to Damian Treffs, Paul Johnson, and John Shea at Routledge for their patience and guidance throughout this process. And I would like to thank the late Robert Nozick, who was General Editor of the *Studies in Ethics* series before he passed away.

I also would like to thank my children, Sophia and Aeryn. They have made my work more pleasant by providing original artwork, both for the walls of my offices and for the pages of many of the books on my bookshelves. (My copy of Harman and Thomson's *Moral Relativism and Moral Objectivity* is quite well illuminated.) And they made going home a pleasure as well. Finally, my greatest debt is to my wife, Catherine, to whom this book is dedicated. Not only did she proofread the entire manuscript, but this book simply would not have been possible without the thoughtful, attentive, and tireless effort she has put into our family. Her help, her support, her patience, and her love have been invaluable.

Introduction

Moral relativism comes in many forms. In the terminology I prefer, the two main forms are Appraiser Relativism, which I address in chapter 1, and Agent Relativism, which I address in chapter 2. I argue that the main arguments for Appraiser Relativism and Agent Relativism are unsuccessful. In chapter 3, I develop a theory of reasons for action based on the ways in which an action can be good as an alternative to the desire-based, agent-centered account I critique in chapter 2.

Appraiser Relativism states that the proposition expressed by a moral sentence varies from context to context in such a way that for any moral sentence and its negation, it is possible for both to be asserted truly.[1] For example, according to Appraiser Relativism, one speaker can assert "Lying is immoral," another speaker can assert "It is not the case that lying is immoral," and both can be making true statements. The main argument for Appraiser Relativism is that it provides the best explanation of the intractability of fundamental moral disagreements. If the parties to those disagreements are both making true statements, then neither side can prove that the other is mistaken. It should come as no surprise, then, that their disagreements are so hard to resolve.

The standard objection to this inference from the best explanation is that Appraiser Relativism runs afoul of our linguistic intuitions about when people are contradicting one another. Fluent speakers of English have the firm linguistic intuition that the assertions made in the example given above are inconsistent with one another. It is, therefore, impossible for both parties to be speaking truly, as required by the Appraiser Relativist's explanation.

In chapter 1, I expand upon this objection in three ways. First, I argue that the class of intuitions that causes trouble for Appraiser Relativism is larger than is usually noticed. For example, I argue that Appraiser Relativism has difficulties accommodating quite firm linguistic intuitions about how moral sentences can be embedded in belief ascriptions, and about whether one person can use a moral sentence to make an assertion about another person's morality.

Second, I argue against three strategies that Appraiser Relativists have recently used to argue that the relevant linguistic intuitions are unreliable. I formulate and defend a general test for assessing the reliability of a certain class of linguistic intuitions, and argue that according to that test, the linguistic intuitions that conflict with Appraiser Relativism's explanation are, in all likelihood, reliable. Because the issue of which intuitions must be respected by our theories is quite a contentious one in philosophy, general principles that allow us to approach this question in a systematic way are valuable additions to the philosopher's toolbox. The test is, therefore, of general interest in any area in which a form of appraiser relativism is maintained, moral or otherwise.[2]

Third, I argue that even if we grant that Appraiser Relativism is true, it still would not provide us with any explanation whatsoever of the intractability of the relevant disagreements. The inference to the best explanation is therefore a nonstarter.

This novel characteristic of the third point is worth stressing. To the best of my knowledge, all of the criticisms of the Appraiser Relativist's (alleged) explanation of moral disagreement have thus far challenged that explanation on the grounds that the truth of Appraiser Relativism would conflict with other claims that we find independently plausible. That is, of course, a perfectly appropriate way to challenge an inference to the best explanation, but it is not often noticed that there is another way to challenge them as well. One can also challenge an inference to the best explanation on the grounds that the truth of the explanans would not explain the explanandum. This possibility means that there is another, previously unexplored way to challenge the main argument for Appraiser Relativism.

One person who mistakenly assumes that an inference to the best explanation can only be challenged in the first way is Christopher Gowans.

Introduction xv

In the introduction to his recent anthology, *Moral Disagreement*, he provides a helpful overview of the debate about moral relativism and the significance of moral disagreement (Gowans 2000). But there also he says that if we concede that the Appraiser Relativist is roughly right about the amount of intractable moral disagreement, then the next step is "to compare the overall plausibility of the objectivist and nonobjectivist accounts" (25). This simply overlooks the possibility that even if Appraiser Relativism turned out to be more plausible than other, objectivist accounts, it still might not explain the intractability of fundamental moral disagreement.

This is a significant point. If we grant that Appraiser Relativism would, if true, explain the intractability of moral disagreement then we do indeed face the very difficult comparative question that Gowans identifies. As Gowans points out, "This is obviously a very large agenda" (Gowans 2000, 25), and will require an overall assessment of both the plausibility of each theory as well as the plausibility of any additional claims that figure in the explanations they provide. But if my argument in chapter 1 is correct, this difficult comparative question can simply be ignored, at least with respect to the main argument for Appraiser Relativism. We do not have to assess the overall plausibility of the explanation provided by Appraiser Relativism because Appraiser Relativism, even if it were true, would not provide us with any explanation whatsoever of the phenomenon in question.

In chapter 2, I examine Agent Relativism, which says, roughly, that there are no universal moral requirements. The main argument for Agent Relativism is that there are always reasons to comply with one's moral requirements, but that the desires to which such reasons must correspond are too capricious for there to be any universal moral requirements. The desires in question are normally taken to be the desires that the agent would have if he were fully rational and fully informed. So the argument posits that for any allegedly universal moral requirement, it is possible to find some moral agent who, despite being fully rational and fully informed, has no desire that would be served by complying with that requirement. If reasons have to be grounded in such desires, and if moral requirements necessarily give rise to or correspond to reasons, then it follows that there are no universal moral requirements.

In response, I argue that the first premise of the Agent Relativist's argument, that if morality requires an agent to do something, then there is a reason for that agent to do that thing, is correct. But depending on how the

Agent Relativist understands the phrase "fully informed," and depending on the relationship between reasons for action, rationality, and motivation, the moral universalist has a number of satisfactory responses to other steps in the Agent Relativist's argument.

Suppose, first, that the Agent Relativist understands the phrase "fully informed" to include information about reasons for action, moral requirements, and the relations between them. Suppose further that it is impossible for a fully rational agent to fail to be moved by what he takes to be a reason for action. I then argue that the Moral Universalist is free to maintain that any fully rational, fully informed agent will have a desire of the relevant kind. So, desires are not too capricious to underwrite universal moral requirements.

Suppose, second, that the Agent Relativist continues to understand the phrase "fully informed" in the same way, but maintains that it *is* possible for a fully rational agent to fail to be moved by what he takes to be a reason for action. I then argue that it is a mistake for the Agent Relativist to infer from the fact that the agent in question lacks a desire of the relevant kind the conclusion that there is no reason for him to comply with the moral requirement in question. For it may simply be that there is a reason for the agent to comply with the moral requirement, but the agent simply fails to be moved by that reason.

Finally, suppose that the Agent Relativist understands the phrase "fully informed" to exclude information about morality, reasons for action, and the relations between them, but that it includes all other kinds of information. The Relativist might adopt this understanding because he is attempting to provide a naturalistically acceptable, reductionist account of reasons for action. In this case, I argue that a naturalistically acceptable account of reasons for action need not suppose that reasons are grounded in the desires of a fully informed, fully rational agent, so understood. On any of the alternatives, the Moral Universalist has an adequate response to the Agent Relativist's argument.

The conclusions I argue for in chapter 2 are not especially novel. Michael Smith is one prominent philosopher who has recently argued against Agent Relativism (Smith 1994). His argument, though, like many others in this area, depends on what seem to me hopelessly inflated claims about the relationships between moral requirements, rationality, reasons for action, desires, and motivation. For instance, Smith holds the view, roughly, that there is a reason for an agent to perform an action if and only if the agent would desire to perform it were he fully rational, and he argues that Agent Relativism is false because all fully rational agents have the same desires (Smith 1994, 150–174). Universal desires can thus underwrite universal reasons, which can, in turn, underwrite universal moral requirements. Along the way, Smith is required to suppose that any agent with any false beliefs is less than fully rational (156), a supposition that is patently false. And in the end, Smith is forced to claim that no fully rational agent would want to be a successful criminal (195), an example of the kind of person whom Gilbert Harman claims could be fully rational without being motivated to comply with what many of us take to be universal moral requirements. I won't argue here that these claims are hopelessly inflated; suffice it to say that I think it a virtue of my arguments in chapter 2 that they rely on minimal, and consequently much more plausible, assumptions. The reader will have to judge the extent to which my arguments are successful.

If reasons for action are not grounded in the desires we would have if we were fully informed and fully rational, what are they grounded in? In chapter 3, I explore an analysis of reasons for action based on the ways in which an action can be good or bad that provides a promising account. Drawing primarily on recent work that rejects goodness *simpliciter* in favor of what Judith Jarvis Thomson calls "the ways of being good," I argue that there is much to be said for this analysis, and that it provides a promising explanation of why there are always reasons for agents to comply with their moral requirements. In the end, though, I conclude that it is possible for an action to be good in certain ways even though there is no reason to perform it. I give examples of actions that are aesthetically good, that are good for artifacts, and that are good for use as an example of something that only an obsessive person would do. But the fact that these actions are good in these ways does not, by itself, give rise to a reason to perform them.

Other ways of being good, though, seem to necessarily give rise to reasons for action. I refer to these ways of being good as *necessarily normative*. Being just and being good for a person are presumably necessarily normative. In an attempt to account for this fact, I explore the concept of intrinsic value, but conclude that once we have given up goodness *simpliciter*, it is doubtful whether the concept of intrinsic value is of much use.

Although chapter 3 is the least conclusive of the three, I view it as a useful attempt to work out the implications of some of the most interesting recent developments in metaethics.

Moral Relativism and Reasons for Action

Chapter 1

Appraiser Relativism and the Reliability of Our Linguistic Intuitions

1 APPRAISER RELATIVISM DEFINED

1.1   Moral relativism takes many forms, and people are motivated to adopt the different forms for different reasons. One prominent form is *Appraiser Relativism*, according to which the proposition expressed by a moral sentence varies from context to context. Appraiser Relativism is primarily motivated by the argument that it provides the best explanation of the intractability we see surrounding fundamental moral disagreements. Those who object to this argument concede that if Appraiser Relativism were true, it would provide an explanation of intractable moral disagreement, but they argue that its explanation conflicts with our linguistic intuitions about when people are contradicting one another. It is commonly assumed that this objection, which might be considered the standard objection, is a conclusive rebuttal of this argument for Appraiser Relativism.

In fact, the standard objection is inconclusive. The two most prominent contemporary Appraiser Relativists, Gilbert Harman and David Wong, have suggested a number of strategies for explaining away our linguistic intuitions, and these strategies have yet to be challenged in the literature. In this chapter, I will examine these strategies in detail, develop a general test for determining the reliability of the relevant class of linguistic intuitions, and argue that the intuitions that conflict with Appraiser Relativism are, in all likelihood, reliable. Moreover, I will argue that the class of linguistic intuitions that undermine Appraiser Relativism is much larger than has previously been noticed. And finally, I argue that even if we were to grant the truth of Appraiser Relativism, it would still not provide us with any explanation whatsoever of the intractability of fundamental moral disagreement. I conclude with some remarks on how my arguments raise doubts not only about the standard argument for Appraiser Relativism, but also about Appraiser Relativism itself.

1.2   Given a sentence, S, we can prefix 'It is not the case that' to S to form what I will call its *syntactic negation*. The distinctive claim of the Appraiser Relativist is that for any moral sentence and its syntactic negation, it is possible for both to be asserted truly.[1] In order to avoid contradiction, then, the Appraiser Relativist needs to tell a story according to which the logical form of moral sentences differs from their grammatical form, and the most plausible story for the Appraiser Relativist to tell is that the moral properties figuring in propositions expressed by moral sentences have an extra argument place, the value of which varies from context to context. So, although one might have thought that the property of being immoral was a one-place property, which a particular action either has or does not have, in fact, there is no such one-place property. Rather, there is the two-place relation of being immoral relative to a morality, and any particular action bears this relation to some moralities, but not to others. Compare: there is no one-place property of being tall, which a particular person either has or does not have. Rather, there is the two-place relation of being tall relative to a comparison class. A person can bear this relation of being tall to some comparison classes (e.g., jockeys), and not bear this relation to other comparison classes (e.g., basketball players).

Two versions of Appraiser Relativism are prominent in the literature. Shifting from the material mode to the formal mode, and letting

(S) Lying is immoral.

be our representative moral sentence, we can define the first version of Appraiser Relativism as follows:

> Speaker Relativism: If M is the morality belonging to the speaker in context C, then the proposition that (S) expresses in C is that lying is immoral relative to M.

This version is called "Speaker Relativism" because it claims that the morality that figures in the proposition expressed is always the morality of the speaker.[2]

The second version of Appraiser Relativism can be defined as follows:

> Salience Relativism: If M is the morality salient to the speaker in context C, then the proposition that (S) expresses in C is that lying is immoral relative to M.

This version is called "Salience Relativism" because it claims that the morality that figures in the proposition expressed is always the morality salient to the speaker.[3] When I use the term "Appraiser Relativism," I intend that to include both Speaker Relativism and Salience Relativism.

A few remarks about the definitions are in order. First, I am not going to say much about what a morality is, or about what marks one morality rather than another as belonging to or being salient to a speaker. I will just be using moralities as placeholders for whatever it is that a relativist believes that moral properties are relative to. For all I have said, the morality that figures in the proposition a speaker asserts might be a function of the moral attitudes predominant in his society, a function of what would be in the interests of his society, a function of his own moral attitudes, or a function of what would be in his own best interests. On such a broad understanding of what might count as a morality, Speaker Relativism includes what is usually known as subjectivism, as well as the more common conventionalist version of Appraiser Relativism that states that the morality that figures in the proposition asserted is a function of the norms of the speaker's society. Second, it is important to realize that these definitions are about the propositions actually expressed by moral sentences, and they are not about which propositions speakers intend to express using moral sentences. Appraiser Relativism is not itself a claim about speaker's intent.[4]

Both Speaker Relativism and Salience Relativism are forms of *cognitive appraiser relativism*. They are *cognitive* theories because, according to them, (S) expresses a proposition (even though it will express different propositions in different contexts). The obvious contrast here is with noncognitivism, according to which (S) does not express a proposition, but rather expresses a prescription or an emotion. Both versions of relativism are forms of what David Lyons calls *appraiser relativism* (Lyons 1976, 211–212) because, they state that the morality that figures in the proposition expressed is determined by facts about the context of the speaker doing the appraising, rather than by facts about the context of the agent performing the action that the speaker appraises. Appraiser Relativism needs to be sharply distinguished from what Lyons calls *agent relativism*, which states that the morality that figures in the proposition expressed is determined by facts about the agent who is being appraised. Thus, the view that it would be wrong for an agent to perform an action just in case that action would be prohibited by the agent's morality is a form of Agent Relativism, not Appraiser Relativism. The important fact to note is that an Agent Relativist cannot try to explain persistent moral disagreement by claiming that both parties to the disagreement are speaking truly. For according to the Agent Relativist, if one person asserts "Smith's lying was immoral," and another asserts "It is not the case that Smith's lying was immoral," then they cannot both be speaking truly. Smith's morality either prohibits that act of lying or it does not.

2 The Alleged Explanation of the Intractability of Moral Disagreements

2.1   How does the Appraiser Relativist explain the intractable disagreements we see surrounding fundamental moral issues? Appraiser Relativists are often sketchy on the details, but presumably their strategy will be to, first, identify some goal that people who are engaged in moral disagreements are trying to achieve, second, show that those people cannot meet that goal, and third, show that those people are unaware that they cannot meet that goal; this is what explains why they keep disagreeing.

According to the Appraiser Relativist, what is the goal of people who are engaged in moral disagreement? Each party to the disagreement is trying to establish the truth of his own assertion. But if both parties think that their assertions are inconsistent with one another, then they cannot believe they have accomplished that goal until the assertion of the other party is shown to be false. Thus, one of their goals is to show that the assertion of the other party is false. However, according to the Appraiser Relativist, this cannot be done because both parties to these disagreements are in fact speaking truly. How is that possible? According to the Appraiser Relativist, the proposition expressed by a moral sentence varies from context to context, and so it follows that for any moral sentence and its syntactic negation, it is possible for both sentences to be asserted truly.[5]

The Appraiser Relativist then argues that it is precisely in those intractable moral disagreements, where the parties seem reasonable and well-informed, that we often find two people speaking truly, even though one person is asserting a moral sentence and the other person is asserting that sentence's syntactic negation. In short, the Appraiser Relativist's explanation is that as long as both parties adhere to the view that their assertions are contradictory, neither party will consider the disagreement resolved until each one has shown the other's assertion to be false. But because both assertions are true, this cannot be done.

The question I will consider, then, is whether the Appraiser Relativist's explanation is the best explanation of the intractable moral disagreements that we see surrounding fundamental moral issues.

One can object to an explanation in two ways. First, one can object by arguing that the truth of the explanans conflicts with other claims we find independently plausible. For example, it may be granted that the trajectories of medium-sized dry goods moving at slow speeds would be explained by Newtonian physics. Nonetheless, because Newtonian physics conflicts with other claims for which we have independent evidence, we have independent grounds for rejecting any explanatory claims made on its behalf. This is the form that the standard objection to Appraiser Relativism takes. Second, one can object to an explanation by arguing that even if the explanans were true, its truth would still not explain the truth of the explanandum in question. For example, it may be granted that the claim that I am wearing a tie does not conflict with other claims we find independently plausible. Nonetheless, we may doubt that the truth of the claim that I am wearing a tie is what explains why I have hazel eyes. The truth of the claim that I am wearing a tie does not stand in any explanatory relation to the truth of the claim that I have hazel eyes.

Let us now turn to an objection of the first kind: that Appraiser Relativism conflicts with other claims we find independently plausible.

3 Some Counterintuitive Implications of Appraiser Relativism

3.1 Many philosophers have become frustrated with the inability of noncognitivism to explain how moral sentences figure in truth-ascriptions and belief-ascriptions, and so they have turned to some form of cognitivist relativism as an attractive alternative. James Dreier, for example, emphasizes this advantage of his version of Appraiser Relativism:

> On my proposed analysis, sentences containing moral terms straightforwardly express propositions—though which propositions they express will vary with the context. So I can simply say that such sentences embed into the relevant contexts just as any other indexical sentences do. (Dreier 1990, 15)

Setting aside the question of whether noncognitivism can explain how moral sentences are embedded into the relevant contexts, I would like to point out here that supposing that moral sentences embed into the relevant contexts just as any other indexical sentences do yields highly counterintuitive implications. To illustrate, first, I will consider four counterintuitive implications shared by both Speaker Relativism and Salience Relativism, and second, I will examine one counterintuitive implication specific to each form of relativism.

The first counterintuitive difficulty common to both Speaker Relativism and Salience Relativism is the standard objection that they conflict with our intuitions about when people's assertions are inconsistent. Whenever two people argue and one of them utters a moral sentence that does not, on its face, contain any context sensitive terms such as indexicals or demonstratives, and the other person utters that sentence's syntactic negation, it seems quite obvious that the two people are contradicting one another. Lyons puts the point nicely:

> The judgments made [by people engaging in moral disagreement] appear to be logically incompatible.... Appearances can be misleading, of course, but the relevant considerations are not negligible; they involve not merely surface grammar but also the conviction shared by laymen and philosophers that only one of these judgments could possibly be right.... (Lyons 1976, 210)

To see the second counterintuitive implication common to both Speaker Relativism and Salience Relativism, suppose Albert utters

(S) Lying is immoral.

And suppose that upon hearing Albert's assertion, Bertrand utters

(S1) That is true. Lying is immoral.

We have the intuition that the fact that Bertrand asserted (S1) in response to Albert's assertion of (S) implies that the proposition to which Bertrand ascribed truth by uttering 'That is true' is identical to the proposition that he then went on to assert by uttering 'Lying is immoral.' But this intuition is inconsistent with both Speaker Relativism and Salience Relativism. For it may have been that Albert and Bertrand had different moralities, or that different moralities were salient to them when they made their assertions, in which case the proposition to which Bertrand ascribed truth by uttering 'That is true' is different from the proposition that he then went on to assert by uttering 'Lying is immoral'.

To see the third and fourth counterintuitive implications, suppose that Albert and Bertrand both utter

(S) Lying is immoral.

We have the intuition that Albert and Bertrand asserted the same proposition. But again, this intuition is inconsistent with Speaker Relativism and Salience Relativism. For it may have been that Albert and Bertrand had different moralities, or that different moralities were salient to them when they made their assertions, in which case the propositions asserted are different.

We also have a fourth intuition, related to the third, that the fact that both Albert and Bertrand uttered (S) implies that both Albert and Bertrand asserted the proposition that lying is immoral. But this, too, is inconsistent with both forms of relativism. If, according to Appraiser Relativism, the fact that they both uttered (S) does not imply that Albert and Bertrand asserted the same proposition (as I argued in the previous paragraph), then, according to Appraiser Relativism, the fact that they both uttered (S) does not imply of any proposition that they both asserted it. *A fortiori*, according to Appraiser Relativism, the fact that they both uttered (S) does not imply of the proposition that lying is immoral that they both asserted it.

As I mentioned, the standard objection to Appraiser Relativism is that it conflicts with our intuitions about when people genuinely disagree. However, these last two counterintuitive implications show something that has not been widely recognized, that Appraiser Relativism conflicts with our intuitions about when people genuinely agree as well. Moreover, these last two implications are instances of a more general problem for Appraiser Relativism: Appraiser Relativism carves up the space of moral propositions in a counterintuitive way, associating a moral sentence such as 'Lying is immoral', not with the one proposition that lying is immoral, but rather with an infinite number of propositions. This means that not only will Appraiser Relativism yield counterintuitive implications for cases involving when two people *said* the same thing, but it will also yield counterintuitive implications in cases involving when two people *believed* the same thing, or *feared* the same thing, or *desired* the same thing, or *hoped* for the same thing, and so on, for each propositional attitude.

3.2   Consider now a counterintuitive implication that is specific to Speaker Relativism. Consider how (S2) can be embedded in (S3):

(S2) Albert is taller than I am.

(S3) Bertrand believes that Albert is taller than I am.

The proposition expressed by (S2) in a context will be, in part, about the speaker in that context, and this remains true even when (S2) occurs as part of a belief ascription.[6] Thus, the proposition that (S3) expresses in a context is, in part, about the speaker in that context, even though the word that refers to the speaker, 'I', occurs within the 'believes that' operator.

Analogously, if Speaker Relativism is true, then the proposition expressed by

(S) Lying is immoral.

in a context will be, in part, about the morality of the speaker in that context, and this will remain true even if (S) occurs as part of a belief ascription. So Speaker Relativism implies that when (S) is embedded into a belief ascription such as

(S4) Bertrand believes that lying is immoral.

the proposition that (S4) expresses in a context will be, in part, about the speaker's morality. Thus, Speaker Relativism implies that when a speaker asserts (S4), the speaker thereby ascribes a belief, namely, the belief that Bertrand believes that lying is immoral relative to the speaker's morality, to Bertrand that is, in part, about the speaker's morality. But that seems manifestly false. Our linguistic intuitions clearly allow that a speaker's assertion of

(S4) could be true even if Bertrand had no beliefs about the speaker's morality.

3.3   Let me now draw your attention to an intuition that Judith Thomson appeals to against Gilbert Harman in (Harman and Thomson 1996), which causes a problem for Salience Relativism.

Recall that according to Salience Relativism, the morality that figures in the proposition expressed by a moral sentence in a context is the morality that was salient to the speaker in that particular context. So if Salience Relativism is true, it ought to be possible for a speaker to utter a moral sentence and thereby assert that something is moral or immoral relative to someone else's morality. But what would such a context be like? I know of no relativist who actually describes such a context. However, Thomson suggests, plausibly enough, that a Salience Relativist might have us look at contexts in which one person is reporting on someone else's morality (Harman and Thomson 1996, 203–204).

Thomson goes on to stress, however, that people do not normally assert that something is moral or immoral relative to someone else's morality by uttering a moral sentence. Rather, they do so by uttering a larger sentence in which the moral sentence is embedded. For example, if I want to report on Albert's morality, I would utter a sentence such as:

(S5) Albert believes that lying is immoral.

and it is not by uttering the embedded sentence 'lying is immoral' that I assert a proposition about what is immoral relative to Albert's morality. Rather, it is by uttering the entire sentence, including the 'Albert believes that' operator. So normal belief ascription contexts do not provide the context that the Salience Relativist requires.

The Salience Relativist might respond to Thomson's objection by drawing attention to the following context. Suppose that Bertrand asks you, 'Does Albert believe that lying is moral or that lying is immoral'? Not wanting to waste your breath, you might respond by uttering

(S) Lying is immoral.

We might call these sorts of contexts, in which a sentence occurs within the scope of an operator, even though it occurs in a different sentence from the original operator, *truncated contexts*. Perhaps the Salience Relativist would say that these truncated contexts are the sort of contexts he had in mind.

But this really won't do at all. One does not assert the proposition expressed by a sentence when that sentence occurs within the scope of a belief operator, and in the above example of a truncated context, the utterance of (S) occurs within the scope of a belief operator. The fact that it was Bertrand instead of you who uttered the word 'believes' is simply irrelevant. Yet once truncated contexts are ruled out, it is difficult to think of any context in which it is intuitively plausible to suppose that by uttering a moral sentence a speaker asserts that something is moral or immoral relative to someone else's morality.

The Salience Relativist could say that it is always a speaker's own morality that is salient to him when he utters a moral sentence. This would explain why there are no contexts in which a speaker asserts a proposition about what is moral or immoral relative to someone else's morality by uttering a moral sentence. But it would be unacceptably *ad hoc*. It would be analogous to trying to explain why one cannot utter the sentence 'I am twelve years old' and thereby assert a proposition about someone else's age, by saying that even though 'I' really refers to whomever happens to be salient to the speaker at the time of assertion, it is only used when the speaker is salient to himself. It is much more plausible to say that it is part of the meaning of 'I' that it always refers to the speaker.

3.4 So both forms of relativism are inconsistent with our intuitions about when people's assertions of moral sentences are inconsistent, they are inconsistent with our intuitions about truth ascriptions, and with our intuitions about the relations between sincere assertions of moral sentences and moral beliefs. Moreover, Speaker Relativism is inconsistent with our intuitions about the content of third-person moral belief attributions. And Salience Relativism conflicts with our intuitions about whether it is possible to assert that something is moral or immoral relative to someone else's morality by uttering a moral sentence. In short, neither form of relativism fits well with many other claims that we find independently plausible.

4 THE FIRST TWO STRATEGIES FOR EXPLAINING AWAY OUR LINGUISTIC INTUITIONS

4.1   The Appraiser Relativist will undoubtedly reply that the intuitions described in the previous section are simply unreliable, and that they can be explained away on grounds that are consistent with Appraiser Relativism. I propose to look at three recent strategies for explaining away the relevant intuitions, one suggested by Wong and two suggested by Harman.[7] Since Appraiser Relativists typically focus on the counterintuitive implications of their view regarding when moral assertions are consistent, the strategies address that implication directly; but I assume that if the strategies were successful in that regard, they would also explain away the other problematic intuitions.

4.2   Let us restrict our attention to moral sentences that do not, on their faces at least, contain any context sensitive terms such as indexicals (e.g., 'I', 'me', 'you') or demonstratives (e.g., 'this', 'that'). The first strategy begins by taking notice of the fact that even though both forms of relativism imply that assertions of sentences such as

(S) Lying is immoral.

and

(~S) It is not the case that lying is immoral.

need not always be inconsistent, they leave open the possibility that they sometimes are. The Appraiser Relativist might then be able to plausibly claim that the range of contexts within which we normally practice moral discourse is such that an assertion of a moral sentence is almost always inconsistent with an assertion of its syntactic negation. The Appraiser Relativist could then plausibly claim that we mistakenly (but understandably) overgeneralize to conclude that it is simply impossible for an assertion of a moral sentence to be consistent with an assertion of its syntactic negation. Let us call this strategy "Overgeneralization."

Wong employs Overgeneralization in his explanation of why most people believe that the parties to moral disagreements are contradicting one another. They fail to realize, he says, that different moralities (what Wong calls the speaker's "moral system") figure in the two parties' assertions, believing instead that the same morality figures in both. If that is so, then Speaker Relativism implies that the two propositions really are inconsistent. Wong puts the point as follows:

> I will argue . . . that what constitutes human fulfillment varies with different groups and societies, and that such variation results in different extensions for 'adequate moral system' as the term is used among different groups and societies. *If this kind of variation exists, it is not difficult to explain why absolutists should fail to recognize it.* Our conceptions of what constitutes human fulfillment are to a large extent shaped by our personal experience, observations of those around us, and what we are taught on the subject. Relatively few of us have been in the position of being pressed to confront an alien conception of human fulfillment and to understand it. (Italics added; Wong 1984, 79)

Wong's explanation seems to be that whenever "what constitutes human fulfillment" is the same for two people, those two people will share the same morality, and hence, if one of those people asserts a moral sentence and the other asserts that sentence's syntactic negation, their assertions really will be inconsistent. Because we rarely encounter people for whom "what constitutes human fulfillment" is not the same as it is for us, it will rarely be the case that an assertion of a moral sentence will be consistent with an assertion of that sentence's syntactic negation. Thus, we can utilize Overgeneralization to explain why we mistakenly think that it is impossible for any assertion of a moral sentence to be consistent with any assertion of that sentence's syntactic negation.

But Wong's attempt to utilize Overgeneralization fails, and the reason why it fails is that the disagreements in need of explanation are quite common and widespread. Wong cites disagreements about abortion (Wong 1984, 190–197) and disagreements about welfare, taxes, and property rights (146–153). Harman also cites those disagreements, and adds to the list issues about the moral status of animals, euthanasia, and our duties to aid others. Harman recognizes, but Wong seems to ignore, that intractable disagreements over these matters occur not only between different societies, but also within societies, and even within families (Harman and Thomson 1996, 10–11). So it is not even remotely plausible to suggest both that what underlies these disagreements is that the parties have different moralities and that people rarely encounter someone with a morality other than their own.

Wong and Harman clearly think that much of the evidence for Appraiser Relativism comes from its ability to explain the intractability of the disagreements just mentioned. But what if an Appraiser Relativist were willing to forego this support for his theory, say, by restricting his relativistic explanation to disagreements that arise between cultures that have very little contact with one another?

I do not think that limiting the range of disagreements will help the Appraiser Relativist. Even if it were rare for an assertion of a moral sentence to be consistent with an assertion of its syntactic negation, our linguistic intuitions would nonetheless reflect these rare cases, and we would not be tempted to overgeneralize. Consider the sentence 'Dogs dogs fight fight'. Many people find it intuitively obvious that there are no contexts in which that sentence is syntactically acceptable. But when you point out a context in which the speaker is using that sentence to say that dogs that dogs fight, also fight, the intuition goes away. Or consider a more germane example: upon canvassing the possible contexts in which one person asserts 'Mother Theresa is a good person' and another person asserts 'It is not the case that Mother Teresa is a good person', it may seem as if those assertions are inconsistent in any possible context. But once you point out a context in which the first person is discussing who is a good person for helping the poor and sick, and the second person is discussing who is a good person to recruit for a professional basketball team, the intuition goes away.

Our intuition that something is impossible is much more sensitive to counterexamples than it is to confirming instances. So we should expect, then, that the particular intuition that it is impossible for an assertion of a moral sentence to be consistent with an assertion of that sentence's syntactic negation to be much more sensitive to counterexamples than to confirming instances. Hence, even if the Appraiser Relativist were to claim that in only rare contexts was an assertion of a moral sentence consistent with an assertion of its syntactic negation, I think that people who were aware of such contexts would be intuitively sensitive to them. Consequently, they would not be tempted to overgeneralize. But it cannot be denied that many people who are aware of such contexts nonetheless find the Appraiser Relativist's claim about consistency to be counterintuitive.

4.3   The second strategy for explaining away our linguistic intuitions is suggested by Harman when he constructs an analogy from physics involving the relativity of mass (Harman and Thomson 1996, 13). Someone who possessed the concept of mass but who was not familiar with the theory of relativity would almost certainly believe that any assertion of a sentence of the form 'X has a mass of 100 grams' would be inconsistent with any assertion of a sentence of the form 'It is not the case that X has a mass of 100 grams'. But Harman tells us that we now know, thanks to Einstein, that "an object can have one mass in relation to one [spatio-temporal] framework and a different mass in relation to another" (ibid., 3). So Harman could say that whatever it is that explains why our intuitions are unreliable in the mass case is also what explains why our intuitions are unreliable in the moral case. Let us call this strategy "Mass."

But what is it that explains why our intuitions are unreliable in the mass case? Harman does not tell us. It seems to me that the reason why a person who had the concept of mass might nonetheless persist in believing that mass is not relative is that the variation in mass between one spatio-temporal framework and another is only detectable (given the accuracy and precision of normal measuring instruments) if those spatio-temporal frameworks are moving at a relative speed approaching the speed of light. But Einstein himself noted in 1920 that "the changes in energy . . . to which we can subject a system are not large enough to make themselves perceptible as a change in the inertial mass of the system" (Einstein 1961, 47). Thus, no matter which spatio-temporal framework a person takes a mass measurement relative to, he always seems to get exactly the same result. We can therefore explain why people's intuitions are unreliable in the mass case by pointing out that it is easy to equate two mass measurements that are, by normal means, indiscernible.

If we think of people who engage in moral discussions as attempting to "measure the moral qualities" of something (for example, the person engaging in a discussion about abortion can be thought of as attempting to measure the heinousness or permissibility of abortion), then Mass would say that our intuitions are unreliable in the moral case because the moralities relative to which people normally measure the moral qualities of a thing always yield moral qualities that are, by normal means, indiscernible, and so, people are unaware that there is any relativity involved.

But when it is fully explained, Mass clearly fails. It is not the case that the moralities relative to which people normally measure moral qualities all yield moral qualities that are indiscernible. Who could equate the moral permissibility attributed to most abortions by liberals with the moral heinousness attributed to those same abortions by conservatives?

5 A TEST FOR DETERMINING THE RELIABILITY OF OUR LINGUISTIC INTUITIONS

5.1   Before I turn to the third strategy for explaining away our intuitions, it will pay to see that both Mass and Overgeneralization make use of an implicit test for determining the reliability of our intuitions.

To state the test in a general form, let us adopt the following terminology. Let us say that a sentence is *incomplete* if and only if it expresses a proposition to the effect that an *n*-place relation holds, even though the sentence itself contains fewer than *n* referring expressions.[8] And when an incomplete sentence is uttered, let us call the object that is not explicitly mentioned in the sentence, but that nonetheless figures in the proposition asserted, *the completing relatum*. So sentences of the form 'The mass of X is M' are incomplete because they express propositions to the effect that a three-place relation holds between an object (referred to by 'X'), a measure (referred to by 'M'), and a spatio-temporal framework. The spatio-temporal framework is the completing relatum. Sentences of the form 'X is taller' are incomplete because they express propositions to the effect that a two-place relation holds between one object (referred to by 'X') and some other object. This other object is the completing relatum. According to Appraiser Relativism, then, moral sentences such as

(S) Lying is immoral.

are incomplete, and a morality is the completing relatum.

We can now state the test:

> Test: The probability that a person's intuitions will be reliable about the logical relations between assertions of incomplete sentences and their syntactic negations is proportional to the probability that he or she is aware that what is being measured varies relative to different completing relata.

5.2   Wong's strategy, Overgeneralization, and Harman's first strategy, Mass, only make sense if they are viewed as implicitly relying on Test. Wong's argument was based on the premise that people were generally unaware that there were different moralities against which actions could be morally evaluated. Harman's argument was based on the premise that people were generally unaware that the measurements of moral qualities given by different moralities vary. Both, then, were appealing to the fact that people are generally unaware of the variation which the Appraiser Relativist is so impressed by. Clearly, though, to get from those premises to the conclusion that people's intuitions can be expected to be unreliable, they must appeal to something like Test.

So Harman and Wong are implicitly committed to Test. I think we should be committed to Test as well. It seems intuitively plausible. It gives the correct answer about the cases we have discussed so far. Obviously, it is highly probable that every competent speaker of English will be aware of the fact that relative to different objects, one and the same thing can be shorter than some and taller than others. So Test yields the intuitively correct conclusion that it is highly probable that the intuitions of every competent speaker of English will be reliable in the '. . . is taller' case. Obviously, it is highly probable that someone who is not acquainted with Einstein's theory of relativity will be unaware of the fact that relative to different spatio-temporal frameworks, one and the same thing can have different masses. So Test yields the correct conclusion that it is highly probable that such a person will have unreliable intuitions in the mass case. But it is highly *probable* that someone who *is* well versed in Einstein's theory of relativity will be aware of the fact that relative to different spatio-temporal frameworks, one and the same thing can have different masses. Therefore, Test yields the conclusion that it is highly probable that the relevant intuitions of such a person are reliable. And this also seems correct.

In section 7, I will apply Test to the moral case, and argue that it yields the opposite of what the Appraiser Relativist needs it to yield. But first I need to discuss a third strategy for explaining away our linguistic intuitions. If that strategy works, it provides a counterexample to Test.

6 THE THIRD STRATEGY FOR EXPLAINING AWAY OUR LINGUISTIC INTUITIONS

6.1   The third strategy for explaining away our linguistic intuitions is suggested by Harman when he asks us to consider "the ancient question [of] whether the earth moves or the sun moves" (Harman and Thomson 1996, 12). How are we to explain the intractability of the disagreement that this question generated? Harman tells us the following:

> Here the relativistic answer is correct. Motion is a relative matter. Something can be in motion relative to one system of spatio-temporal coordinates and not in motion relative to another. The particular motion an object exhibits will differ from one system to another. There is no such thing as absolute motion, apart from one or another system of coordinates. (Ibid., 12–13)

I take it that Harman is suggesting that the different parties to the ancient disagreement had different spatio-temporal frameworks in mind. This allowed both parties to speak truly and so neither could refute the other. But it took many centuries for the debate to finally be resolved, so they obviously did not realize that they were talking past one other. Harman tells us that an analogous explanation "is also plausible in the moral case" (ibid., 13). So Harman could say that whatever it is that explains why our intuitions are unreliable in the motion case also explains why our intuitions are unreliable in the moral case. Let us call this strategy "Motion."

It is worth noting that neither Overgeneralization nor Mass will explain why the ancient disagreement was so intractable. Overgeneralization will not work because it is often the case that people determine whether something is in motion relative to many different spatio-temporal frameworks, sometimes relative to the earth, sometimes relative to this or that moving vehicle. And Mass will not work because relative to those different frameworks, we get easily noticeable differences in relative speed.

It is also worth noting that if Harman is right, that what explains why the ancient disagreement was so intractable is that both parties to that disagreement were speaking truly while mistakenly believing their assertions to be inconsistent with their opponent's, then we have a counterexample to Test. For precisely those reasons that make Overgeneralization and Mass fail in the motion case, it seems that people should be aware of the fact that relative to different spatio-temporal frameworks, one and the same object can exhibit different motions. Test then implies that people should not believe their assertions are inconsistent when they are not.

6.2   But it seems plain that Harman is mistaken, both in his characterization of the disagreement as one in which both parties were speaking truly, and as to what explains why it took so long for the disagreement to be resolved. After all, modern astronomy teaches us that the disagreement was eventually resolved in favor of those who asserted 'The earth is revolving around the sun' (or some translation thereof), and it is, after all, obvious that motion is relative. It does not take any sophisticated equipment or subtle experiments to realize that the propositions asserted in the following two contexts are consistent. In the first context, the speaker is on a train, and upon observing that his children have stopped racing up and down the aisles, he asserts the sentence 'The children are stationary'. In the second context, a speaker is on the platform and says of the same train 'That train, and the children on it, are moving'.[9]

But if people's linguistic intuitions are reliable in the motion case, then Motion fails. Harman cannot say that what explains the unreliability of our intuitions in the moral case is the same as what explains the unreliability of our intuitions in the motion case if, as I have argued, our intuitions are not unreliable in the motion case.

6.3   The question remains, though, how should we characterize the ancient disagreement, and why did it take so long to be resolved? Obviously this will require some speculation, and given that the disagreement persisted for so long and that there were so many different parties to it, it seems unlikely that there will be any single explanation that applies across the board. Nevertheless, the following story seems plausible.

One reason Aristotle would have asserted (a translation of) "The earth is stationary" is that he was aware of the fact that there was no discernible *stellar parallax* (Abell 1982, 18).[10] Parallax is the degree of shift in the apparent position of an object as a result of the object's motion relative to an observer, and stellar parallax is the degree of shift in the apparent position of a star as a result of the earth's motion relative to that star. To illustrate a simple case of parallax, imagine that you put this book down at a distance of two feet directly in front of you, and then move two feet to one side. The parallax between the apparent position of the book when it was directly in front of you and after you moved two feet to one side would be forty-five degrees. If you were to place the book down at a distance of four feet directly in front of you, and then move two feet to one side, the parallax would be twenty-two and one-half degrees. The farther the book is from you, the smaller the parallax, and the more it will seem to you as if you have not moved relative to the book.

Aristotle reasoned that if the earth revolved around the sun, there would be a stellar parallax between the apparent position of the stars when the earth was on one side of the sun and the apparent position of the stars when the earth was on the other side of the sun. However, because the stars are so far away, Aristotle's contemporaries could not discern any stellar parallax whatsoever. Aristotle was aware of this fact, and so he asserted "The earth is stationary." Knowing that the sun and the earth were in motion relative to each other, Aristotle then asserted "The sun revolves around the earth."

A measure of stellar parallax is a measure of a relation between an observer and a star, and so it seems reasonable to speculate that when Aristotle asserted 'The earth is stationary' and 'The sun revolves around the earth', he was implicitly taking the stars against which he was measuring the stellar parallax as defining his reference frame. That the earth was stationary with respect to the stars and that the sun was in motion with respect to the stars was a perfectly reasonable view for Aristotle to have held, given that the stellar parallax was indiscernible. Indeed, even with the improved instruments of the sixteenth century, Tycho Brahe was still unable to detect any stellar parallax, and used this fact as an argument against those who asserted "The earth is moving." While Brahe acknowledged that the stellar parallax would be undetectable if the stars were very far away, astronomers still thought of the stars as lying just outside of Saturn. At such a close distance, stellar parallax would have been discernible with Brahe's instruments (Hoskins 1997b, 111).

In the eighteenth century, astronomers determined by other methods that some stars were at least four-hundred-thousand times as far away from the earth as the earth is from the sun, and in the nineteenth century, stellar parallax was finally detected by Wilhelm Struve, and then by Friedrich Bessel (Hoskins 1997c, 219). Thus, Aristotle's view has been shown to be false.

However, as early as the seventeenth century, astronomers were beginning to understand that the motions of the sun and the earth were explained by gravitational forces, and so it became common to take the more massive sun as defining their reference frame (ibid., 210). And modern astronomers do roughly the same thing: they take the center of mass of the earth-sun system as defining their reference frame because it is towards this center of mass that both the earth and the sun are constantly accelerating as they orbit about each other. George Abell, for example, says that because the mass of the sun is approximately 300,000 times the mass of the earth,

> the common center of mass of the earth-sun system must be less than 1/300,000 of the distance from the center of the sun to the center of the earth. This puts it well inside the surface of the sun. Essentially, then, the earth revolves around the sun.[11] (Abell 1982, 109)

This story seems quite plausible, but it stands in stark contrast with the story that Harman would have us accept about intractable moral disagreements. Harman would have us accept that what explains the intractable moral disagreements we see is that the parties to it are both speaking truly. But it is wrong to say that both parties to the ancient disagreement about the earth and the sun spoke truly. Scientific investigation has shown that the ancients who asserted "The sun revolves around the earth" spoke falsely. What explains why it took so long to show that they spoke falsely is simply that it took that long to develop sufficiently precise instruments and a better understanding of the gravitational forces underlying celestial mechanics. But surely Harman is not suggesting that intractable moral disagreements will be resolved by future scientific investigation and technological innovation.

6.4   In summary, the three strategies intended to explain away our intuitions regarding the logical relations between assertions of moral sentences do not succeed. Overgeneralization fails because the disagreements in need of explanation are common and widespread. Mass fails because the moralities that people normally use to measure the moral qualities of something yield moral qualities that are easily discernible. Finally, Motion fails because it simply is not true that our intuitions are unreliable about the logical relations between assertions of sentences about motion.

7 APPRAISER RELATIVISM, EXPLANATION, AND THE RELIABILITY OF OUR LINGUISTIC INTUITIONS

7.1   In section 3, I examined how well the truth of Appraiser Relativism would fit in with other claims that we find independently plausible. I will now turn to the question of how well the truth of Appraiser Relativism would explain the moral disagreements it purports to explain.

7.2   Once Test has been explicitly delineated, it seems quite plausible to think that if either form of Appraiser Relativism were true and moral sentences really were incomplete, Test would show that it is highly probable that people's intuitions are reliable about the logical relations between the assertions of moral sentences. Contrary to Wong's suggestion, most people have had contact with many different moralities. Contrary to Harman's suggestion, the different moralities with which people normally have contact display dramatically different moral qualities for the same action. But if these moral qualities differ dramatically from one another, then surely people would notice these dramatic differences as soon as they encountered them. To maintain otherwise would be akin to saying that an astronaut who has made multiple trips to the moon remained unaware of the fact that the weight of an object varies with respect to gravitational fields. It is possible, but highly unlikely.

So if Appraiser Relativism were true, then it would be highly probable that people would be aware of the fact that the moral qualities of something vary relative to different moralities. Test, then, implies that if Appraiser Relativism were true, it would be highly probable that people's intuitions would be reliable about when parties to a moral disagreement were really contradicting one another.

Recall now that Appraiser Relativism's explanation of the apparent intractability of moral disagreements about capital punishment, abortion, euthanasia, and so on, relied on the fact that the parties to those disagreements persisted in mistakenly believing that their assertions were inconsistent with each other. This is what provided the impetus for refuting the opposing party's assertion, which could not be done, according to the Appraiser Relativist, because the assertion of the opposing party was in fact true. But if, as I have argued, Appraiser Relativism implies that it is highly probable that people's intuitions will be reliable about when their assertions are inconsistent, it also follows that if Appraiser Relativism is true, it is highly *improbable* that people will persist in believing that their assertions are inconsistent with each other when they are not. Furthermore, when they become aware that their assertions are consistent with each other, they will no longer view the refutation of their opponent's view as a prerequisite for establishing their own. Compare: once I realize that you are saying that Mother Theresa is a good person for helping the poor and sick, and I am saying that Mother Theresa is a good person to recruit for a professional basketball team, then I no longer feel the need to refute your view in order to establish my own. Our disagreement is resolved once we realize we are talking past one another. Similarly, parties to the moral disagreement would satisfy themselves with establishing the truth of their own assertions. They could then turn to the quite different question: given that both of their assertions are true, what ought they to do?

In short, if Appraiser Relativism were true, then the very intractability that is in need of explanation would be highly improbable.

7.3   It is a difficult task to determine exactly when the truth of one proposition would provide an explanation of the truth of another, and I offer nothing that approaches a set of necessary and sufficient conditions. However, the following necessary condition seems generally correct:

> Explanation: If the truth of an explanans (Es) would make it highly improbable that an explanandum (Ed) is true, then the truth of (Es) would not explain the truth of (Ed).

To illustrate Explanation, imagine the following case. Suppose that Albert knew that he weighed 150 pounds, but that he lied to his friend by saying that he weighed 130 pounds. We might then wonder what explains the following explanandum:

> (E) Albert lied to his friend in saying that he weighed 130 pounds.

There are many propositions that if true would provide an explanation of (E), although some of the explanations might not be particularly good. Consider

> (P1) Albert is vain.

The truth of (P1) would provide an explanation of (E). However, it might come to light that while (P1) would provide *an* explanation of (E), it would not provide a very good explanation. This might be because, say, 150 pounds is closer to an attractive weight for someone of Albert's height than is 130 pounds. Thus, it might turn out that

> (P2) Albert had a bet with his friend that he would win if, but only if, he weighed 130 pounds.

would provide a better explanation of (E) than would (P1). But either (P1) or (P2) would provide an explanation of (E), even if the explanation provided would not be a particularly good one.

Contrast (P1) and (P2) with

> (P3) In all the years they have known each other, Albert has never lied to his friend.

(P3) would not explain (E). Not only would it not provide a good explanation of (E), it would not provide a *bad* explanation of (E). In fact, it would not provide *any* explanation of (E) whatsoever. The reason why it does not provide any explanation whatsoever is that Explanation is true and the truth of (P3) would make (E) highly improbable.

7.4   I argued that if Appraiser Relativism were true, then the very intractability in need of explanation would be highly improbable. Explanation, then, yields that the truth of Appraiser Relativism would not provide any explanation whatsoever of this intractability of the relevant disagreements. *A fortiori*, even if we were to grant that Appraiser Relativism were true, its truth would not provide the best explanation of the intractability of the relevant disagreements. The argument for Appraiser Relativism based on the premise that it would is therefore unsound.

8   Summary and Concluding Remarks

8.1   I have argued that neither Speaker Relativism nor Salience Relativism can be supported by the claim that it provides the best explanation of the intractable moral disagreements we see surrounding capital punishment, abortion, euthanasia, and other fundamental moral issues. After considering a number of intuitions with which they conflict, I examined three arguments for the conclusion that those intuitions were unreliable, and so could not serve as evidence against Appraiser Relativism. This examination led to two conclusions. First, that the arguments are unsound. Overgeneralization fails because the disagreements that the Appraiser Relativist hopes to explain are common and widespread. Mass fails because it is not the case that the moral assessments characteristic of different moralities are indiscernible. Finally, Motion fails because our intuitions in the motion case are reliable. My second conclusion was that Test provides a good guide for judging the reliability of our intuitions.

I also argued that Appraiser Relativism does not provide the best explanation of the relevant disagreements. Appealing to Test, I argued that if Appraiser Relativism were true, it would be highly probable that people's intuitions about when they were disagreeing would be reliable. So if the parties to a moral disagreement really were talking past one another, as the Appraiser Relativist supposes, the parties would realize that they were. They would then give up trying to refute the other person's view, and the disagreement would be resolved. Thus, if Appraiser Relativism were true, then the very disagreements in need of explanation would be highly improbable. Explanation then implies that Appraiser Relativism does not provide any explanation of those disagreements. *A fortiori,* Appraiser Relativism does not provide the best explanation of those disagreements, and the argument for Appraiser Relativism on the ground that it does provide the best explanation is unsound.

8.2   Of course, this leaves us with the initial question of how to best explain the intractable nature of disagreements we often see surrounding fundamental moral issues. This is a large question. I have no general answer, but can offer the following observations.

First, I think it is doubtful that there is a single explanation that applies to all of the relevant moral disagreements. One reason why disagreements about capital punishment are intractable is that we do not at present have an adequate theory of retributive justice; but our lack in that area plays no role in explaining the intractability of disagreements about abortion. Further, one reason why disagreements about abortion are intractable is that we lack an adequate theory of personhood; but this lack obviously plays no role in explaining the intractability of disagreements about capital punishment. (No one denies that people on death row are *people*.) In short, one should not expect the disagreements of applied ethics to be resolved until the underlying theoretical disagreements are resolved. These underlying theoretical disagreements will vary from issue to issue.

Second, even in the absence of any positive explanation of why moral disagreements tend to be intractable, if the arguments I have given in this paper are sound, we know that both Speaker Relativism and Salience Relativism cannot provide us with any explanation whatsoever.

8.3   Finally, it should be noted that many of the ideas I consider in this chapter question not only the soundness of the argument for Appraiser Relativism, but also the plausibility of Appraiser Relativism itself. Any philosophical theory that runs counter to our pre-theoretical intuitions comes at a cost. If those intuitions cannot be explained away, the cost is even greater. If those intuitions are as firm and as widely held as the intuitions which run counter to Appraiser Relativism are, then I think the cost is very high indeed.

Chapter 2
Agent Relativism and Reasons for Action

Agent Relativism, understood as the thesis that there are no universal moral requirements, is motivated by the thought that while there are always reasons to comply with one's moral requirements, the desires to which such reasons would have to correspond are too capricious for there to be any universal moral requirements. I argue that the Moral Universalist is free to maintain either (i) that any fully rational, fully informed agent *will* have a desire that would be served by complying with what the Moral Universalist takes to be universal moral requirements, and so the desires are *not* too capricious, or (ii) that a naturalistically acceptable account of reasons need not suppose that reasons are grounded in desires. Either way, the Moral Universalist has grounds for rejecting this basis for Agent Relativism.

1 THE PRACTICALITY ARGUMENT FOR AGENT RELATIVISM

1.1   What does it mean to say that there are universal moral requirements? I will take it to mean that there is at least one kind of action such that morality requires every agent to refrain from performing any action of that kind.[1] In the interest of simplicity, I am going to make two assumptions. First, I will assume that refraining from performing an action is itself performing an action. Second, I will dispense with talk of *kinds* of actions and speak instead just of actions, but I will do this with the assumption that two different agents can perform the same action. We can now define Moral Universalism as follows:

> Moral Universalism: There is some action that every agent is morally required to perform.

1.2   I think that Moral Universalism, defined in this way, is true. Some philosophers, though, argue that reflection on the practical nature of morality and on the nature of reasons for action reveals that Moral Universalism is not true, and that we should instead accept its negation, which I will call Agent Relativism.[2] According to Agent Relativism there are no universal moral requirements. That is:

> Agent Relativism: For any action, there is some agent who is not morally required to perform that action.[3]

The argument those philosophers have in mind begins with the claim that reflection on the practical nature of morality reveals that if an agent is morally required to perform an action, then there is a reason for that agent to perform that action. I will call this the Practicality Requirement:

> The Practicality Requirement: For any action, if an agent is morally required to perform that action, then there is a reason for that agent to perform that action.

Next, the Agent Relativist argues that reflection on the way in which reasons for action are based on desires reveals that for any action there is an agent such that there is no reason for that agent to perform that action. Call this Reasons Relativism:

> Reasons Relativism: For any action, there is some agent such that there is no reason for that agent to perform that action.

And Reasons Relativism and the Practicality Requirement entail Agent Relativism. If there were some action that every agent were morally required to perform, then it would follow from the Practicality Requirement that there is a reason for every agent to perform that action (although not necessarily the same reason for every agent). But this is precisely what Reasons Relativism denies.

1.3   Let us call this argument for Agent Relativism, the Practicality Argument. Anyone who sides with Moral Universalism must be able to respond to the Practicality Argument. I will argue that the Practicality Requirement is very plausible, and that Reasons Relativism should be rejected instead. Although my argument against Reasons Relativism relies heavily on intuitions, and so is limited in its appeal to those who share my intuitions, I also examine two arguments on behalf of Reasons Relativism, and conclude that they cannot be successfully used against the Moral Universalist. In the absence of further argument, the Moral Universalist is therefore free to reject the Practicality Argument for Agent Relativism.

2 Two Arguments for Moral Universalism

2.1   Before turning to the Practicality Argument let me address a prior question: why should anyone be attracted to Moral Universalism in the first place? There are two arguments sometimes put forward in its favor, one more persuasive than the other.

The first argument I will call the *Argument from Extreme Heinousness*. According to the Argument from Extreme Heinousness, some actions are simply so heinous that they cannot possibly be morally permitted. Torturing a baby to death for fun is the standard example. But some people think that for any action alleged to be sufficiently heinous, they can conceive of possible circumstances where an agent is forced to choose between performing that action on one person and performing the same action on some absurdly large number of people. In such circumstances, these people say, the consequences of not performing the action in question are themselves so tragic that morality permits, perhaps even requires, that the agent perform the heinous action on one person. If you think, as I do, that numbers can matter, then you are unlikely to be persuaded by the Argument from Extreme Heinousness.

2.2   But there is another argument for Moral Universalism that is more persuasive. This argument begins with the very modest claim that some agent is morally required to perform some action. Now, either all other agents are morally required to perform that action as well, or they are not. If they are, then the requirement is universal, and Moral Universalism is true. But if they are not, then there must be some morally relevant difference between the circumstances of those who are required to do it and the circumstances of those who are not. But then we can construct a more qualified moral requirement that takes this difference into account, and that, in conjunction with the different circumstances, explains the difference in moral requirements. That someone thinks morality exhibits this kind of "relativity to circumstances," as it is sometimes called, does not mark him as an Agent Relativist, but the strategy seems to be perfectly general: *whatever* differences exist between people who are subject to different moral requirements can be noted as being morally relevant. A more qualified moral requirement can then be constructed which applies to everyone. The circumstances that call for the action are "built-in," so to speak, to the moral requirement. Call this argument the *Argument from Morally Relevant Differences*.

Unlike the Argument from Extreme Heinousness, the Argument from Morally Relevant Differences does not require that universal moral requirements be universal because the acts they prohibit are particularly heinous. For example, violating the suitably qualified moral requirement to keep one's promises is not particularly heinous—there are far worse things one could do. Nonetheless, because the requirement takes into account all those circumstances in which one is permitted to break one's promise, violating it is never morally permitted.

2.3   Gilbert Harman, however, says that the Argument from Morally Relevant Differences is invalid. He says that it is possible for two people to be subject to different moral requirements, even though there is no more qualified moral requirement that applies to them both (Harman 1978b). Rather, he says, it might be that the reason why the people are subject to different moral requirements is because the truth of a general metaethical principle places constraints on what morality requires. For example, many people have thought it a plausible metaethical principle that if an action is not within the power of an agent, then the agent is not morally required to perform that action. This is the so-called principle that *ought* implies *can*. So if it turns out that Alfred promised to leap tall buildings, but doing so is not within his power, then he is not morally required to keep his promise. But, Harman says, it may turn out that Superman is morally required to leap a tall building, even though Alfred is not, and that this difference in moral requirements would be explained by the truth of the general metaethical principle cited above, and by the fact that Superman can and Alfred cannot leap tall buildings.

But Harman is mistaken in thinking that this sort of example raises doubt about either Moral Universalism or about the Argument from Morally Relevant Differences. If a morally relevant difference is any difference that makes a difference in what morality requires of agents (and what else could it be?), then the correct view to take is that there is a morally relevant difference between Superman and Alfred, namely, that Superman can leap tall buildings and Alfred cannot. This shows that the moral requirement to keep one's promises needs at least one qualification: one is morally required to keep only those promises that it is within one's power to keep. But, first, that seems true. Second, it is not objectionable to think that universal moral requirements can be suitably qualified to take into account such differences when and where they are relevant. Otherwise, believing in the principle that *ought* implies *can* would mark one as an Agent Relativist, and this surely is not the case.

3 A Defense of the Practicality Requirement

3.1   So I think that Moral Universalism is true. But if Moral Universalism is true, then we need an effective response to the Practicality Argument, because its conclusion—Agent Relativism—is inconsistent with Moral Universalism. Recall that the Practicality Argument has two premises: the Practicality Requirement, which states that if morality requires an agent to perform an action, then there is a reason for that agent to perform that action, and Reasons Relativism, which states that for any action, there is some agent for whom there is no reason to perform that action. The first response to consider is one that denies the Practicality Requirement, and states instead that it is possible for there to be no reason for someone to do what morality requires of him. I will argue, however, that with a proper understanding of the relationship between morality, reasons for action, and what an agent ought to do, denying the Practicality Requirement is implausible.

The Practicality Requirement states that if morality requires an agent to perform an action, there is a reason for that agent to perform that action. That is, there are always reasons to comply with one's moral requirements. But how are we to understand the term 'reason' as it appears in this premise? I intend to understand it as I think it is normally used. As the term 'reason' is normally used, a reason is a consideration in favor of an action. More precisely, a reason for an agent to do something is a consideration in favor of that agent's doing that thing. Reasons, in this sense, connect up with what an agent ought to do. When someone asks *why he ought to do something*, he is asking for the reasons for him to do that thing. He is asking to know what those considerations are that are in favor of his doing that thing. Thus, a reason for an agent to perform an action is a fact that is favorably relevant to its being the case that he ought to do that thing.[4] Of course, there can be both reasons for an agent to do something and reasons for that agent not to do that very same thing. When someone asks *whether he ought to do something*, what he is asking is whether the reasons for him to do it outweigh, are stronger than, or, as I shall put it, *override* the reasons for him not to do it. If they do, and only if they do, then the agent ought to perform the action.

We need to distinguish between there *being* a reason for an agent to do something and an agent's *having* a reason to do something. When an agent has a reason to do something, what the agent takes to be a reason for him to do that thing really *is* a reason for him to do that thing. There are two kinds of cases in which there is a reason for an agent to do something, even though the agent does not have that particular reason as his reason for doing that thing. First, there may be a reason of which the agent is unaware. In that case, the agent will not take it to be a reason. For example, Smith may be unaware that his taking a certain medicine will make him feel better, but that it will make him feel better may still be a reason for him to take the medicine. If Smith takes the medicine at all, then *his* reason for doing so will *not* be that his taking it will make him feel better. Second, there may be a reason that an agent is aware of, but which he simply does not believe is a reason. For example, Jones may be aware that his taking a certain medicine will lower his blood pressure, and unbeknownst to Jones, it may be that his blood pressure is dangerously high, and so there is a reason for him to lower his blood pressure. But if Jones thinks that his blood pressure is just fine, then he will not take the fact that his taking the medicine will lower his blood pressure to be a reason for him to take the medicine. If he takes the medicine at all, *his* reason for doing so will *not* be that his taking it will lower his blood pressure.

Is it possible for there to be a case in which an agent has a reason to do something even though there is no reason for him to do that thing? Not if we understand the relationship between there being a reason and an agent's having a reason as I think we should. I had said that when an agent has a reason to do something, what the agent takes to be a reason for him to do that thing really *is* a reason for him to do that thing. But if there really isn't any reason for, say, Alfred to kiss a certain frog, then no matter what Alfred takes to be a reason for him to kiss the frog, what he takes to be a reason isn't really a reason. Compare: can an agent have evidence for thinking that Jones committed a certain murder if there *is* no evidence for thinking that Jones committed the murder? Intuitively, the answer is no.

We also need to distinguish between the case in which it is rational for an agent to perform an action and the case in which the reasons for the agent to perform the action override the reasons for him not to perform the action. As the word 'rational' is normally used, a person can be perfectly rational in coming to his decision to do something, and yet do what he ought not do, because, say, he has some bad information or is unaware of some relevant fact. For example, the fact that a person was fully rational in coming to his decision to sell some stock at a certain time does not imply that he ought to sell the stock, for it may be that, unbeknownst to him and contrary to all evidence available to him, selling his stock will have disastrous consequences.[5]

3.2   With this understanding of reasons for action and what an agent ought to do in mind, should we be troubled about rejecting the Practicality Requirement and saying instead that it is possible for morality to require an agent to do something even though there is no reason for him to do it?

David Brink suggests that rejecting the Practicality Requirement should not trouble us. Although he is optimistic about the prospects of demonstrating that there are always reasons for an agent to do what morality requires, he suggests that nothing is lost if we cannot always "reproach the immoralist" for doing what he ought not do, for we can still always "reproach the immoralist with immorality" (Brink 1997, 32).

But Brink's suggestion is unsatisfactory. One does not *reproach* the immoralist for acting contrary to morality if one thinks that the immoralist *ought* to be acting contrary to morality, and this is precisely what one would think if one believed that there were overriding reasons for the immoralist to act contrary to morality.

Bernard Williams makes the same mistake in his discussion of the criticisms that can be leveled against someone who cannot be convinced that he ought to be nicer to his wife (Williams 1989, 39-40). Williams asks rhetorically: what more do we need to say about this person over and above saying that the person in question is inconsiderate, brutal, hard, etc.? The answer is that we also want to say that the person *ought not* be inconsiderate, brutal, hard, and so on. We want our saying of these things to be *criticisms,* as they would not be in the mouth of someone who thought that one ought to be inconsiderate, brutal, hard, and so on, towards one's wife.

So Brink's and Williams's suggestion as to why it would be unproblematic to deny the Practicality Requirement is mistaken. Moreover, I think that there are two consequences of denying the Practicality Requirement that show that denying it is problematic.

3.3   If the Practicality Requirement is false, then it is possible for morality to require an agent to do something even though there is no reason for him to do it. But if there is no reason for him to do it, it follows that it is not the case that he ought to do it. He ought to do it only if the reasons for him to do it override the reasons for him not to do it, and we are supposing that there are *no* reasons for him to do it. Thus, if the Practicality Requirement is false, it is possible for morality to require an agent to do something even though it is not the case that he ought to do that thing. That seems counterintuitive: most of us think that if morality requires you to do something, then it follows that you ought to do it.

However, some people think it does not follow that you ought to do it, and welcome this consequence. For example, Williams argues that while there are perhaps very strong reasons for people to comply with their moral requirements, those reasons are overridden by other reasons in some circumstances. He says,

> while we are sometimes guided by the notion that it would be the best of worlds in which morality were universally respected and all men were of a disposition to affirm it, we have in fact deep and persistent reasons to be grateful that that is not the world we have. (Williams 1976, 23)

Before we can decide for or against a view like that of Williams, we would need to explore his claims about the sorts of non-moral reasons that may override moral requirements. A full discussion would take us too far afield here. Suffice it to say that what I find puzzling about Williams's position is that it seems obvious to me that to the extent that these non-moral reasons strike us as weighty enough to override a moral requirement, they also strike us as weighty enough to actually *relieve* us of the moral requirement with which they allegedly conflicted. Morality can require great personal sacrifice, but typically, morality itself allows for other non-moral pursuits and values. And when it doesn't, I, for one, believe that what one ought to do is abide by one's moral requirements. Morality not only allows other non-moral pursuits and values, it allows the right amount of room for them. For this reason, I think it is false to assert that morality can require someone to do something even though there is no reason for that person to do that thing.

3.4   There is a second consequence of denying the Practicality Requirement which I think is even more troubling than the first. A reason for an agent to perform an action is a fact that is favorably relevant to its being the case that he ought to perform that action. Denying the Practicality Requirement requires that one say that in some circumstances, even though it is a fact that morality requires an agent to do something, there are no facts that are favorably relevant to its being the case that he ought to do that thing. It follows that, though morality requires him to do that thing, the fact that it does does not support the case that he ought to do it. But how could that be possible? Surely the moral requirement that an agent do something does, at the very minimum, support the case that he ought to do it.

3.5   What would it take to convince us otherwise? We would have to come to be convinced of an account of the source of morality, or about the source of some aspect of morality, and be convinced that anything coming from that source is not worth caring about. A certain form of moral skepticism, sometimes called *practical skepticism*, would have to be true. (The contrast here is with *cognitive skepticism*.) Christine Korsgaard describes that form as follows:

> The moral sceptic is someone who thinks that the explanation of moral concepts will be one that does not support the claims that morality makes on us. He thinks that once we see what is really behind morality, we won't care about it any more.[6] (Korsgaard 1996, 13–14)

For example, suppose Thrasymachus, of Plato's *Republic*, tried to convince us that his views about the source of morality were true. According to his story, the rulers are enabled by their superior strength and intelligence and are motivated by self-interest to control the upbringing and education of their subjects. They do so in such a way that their subjects grow up believing that they ought to be just and that being just requires compliance with whatever laws are made by the rulers. Further, the laws made by the rulers are crafted solely to serve the interests of those rulers, almost invariably at the expense of the interests of the subjects. Thrasymachus, being the enlightened person that he is, realizes this, and concludes that the subjects should not be just. Indeed, Thrasymachus seems to think that the fact that something is just is a reason *not* to do it, because injustice is always "to one's own profit and advantage" (344c). Thrasymachus, therefore, is an example of someone who rejects the Practicality Requirement.

But Thrasymachus had another option. He could have concluded that justice does not require compliance with the laws made by the rulers. And indeed, that seems right. Justice does not require subjects to abide by the law when the law is crafted solely to serve the interests of the rulers at the expense of the interests of the subjects. So I am not convinced by Thrasymachus's story. The point generalizes this way: whenever someone tries to give an account which implies that a person ought not be just, then the correct response will be to reject that account of justice, not to reject the Practicality Requirement.

Intuition and ordinary usage provide further support for the Practicality Requirement. We do *talk* as if moral requirements are reasons for action. If I say that you should pay back the five dollars you borrowed from Alfred and you ask why, it seems perfectly correct for me to responsd, "Because morality requires you to do so." In saying that, I seem to have stated a reason why you ought to pay back the five dollars. So I think that the defender of Moral Universalism would do well to focus his or her attention on Reasons Relativism, the other premise in the Practicality Argument for Agent Relativism.

4 The Desire Argument for Reasons Relativism

4.1   Recall that Reasons Relativism says that for any action, there is some agent for whom there is no reason to perform that action. I will examine two different arguments for Reasons Relativism. These arguments share the feature that they both connect the reasons for an agent to do something to the desires the agent would have in certain idealized circumstances. I will argue that neither of them are successful against the Moral Universalist, and that a view according to which reasons are often not related to an agent's desires can be in accordance with both naturalistic scruples and with the correct account of the relationship between reasons for action and motivation.

The first argument for Reasons Relativism that I will examine is the Desire Argument:

The Desire Argument

(P1) There is a reason for an agent to perform an action if and only if the agent would, were he fully rational and fully informed, have some desire that would be served by his performing that action.[7]

(P2) For any action, there is some agent who would, despite being fully rational and fully informed, have no desire that would be served by his performing that action.

(C) Hence, for any action, there is some agent for whom there is no reason to perform that action.

My response to the Desire Argument takes the form of a dilemma. I shall argue that if a certain form of internalism, which I call "Reasons Internalism," is true, then the Agent Relativist's argument for (P2) begs the question against the Moral Universalist. But if Reasons Internalism is false, then (P1) is false as well. Either way, the Desire Argument is unsatisfactory.

4.2   The typical argument for (P2) claims that, in those cases with the most plausible examples of actions that a Moral Universalist might claim to be morally required of every agent, it is possible for there to be an agent who (i) is fully informed, (ii) is fully rational, and yet (iii) has no desires that would be served by his compliance with the allegedly universal moral requirement. For example, against the claim that every agent is morally required to refrain from killing innocent people, Harman says that it is possible for there to be a fully rational, fully informed member of "Murder, Incorporated" who has no desires that would be served by his refraining from killing his innocent victims (Harman 1975, 5).

Let us suppose that the name of the member of Murder, Incorporated is "Villain." Harman would have us believe that Villain is fully informed, fully rational, and yet lacks any desire of the relevant kind. But on the most obvious understanding of "fully informed," according to which being informed means, among others things, being informed about reasons for action, it can be shown that this description of Villain begs the question against the defender of Moral Universalism.

4.3   My argument that this description of Villain begs the question relies on a general principle, which I will call "Moral Internalism," that places constraints on the desires of fully informed, fully rational agents. The principle says if an agent (i) is fully informed, (ii) is morally required to perform some action, and yet (iii) has no desire that would be served by performing that action, then he is not fully rational.

The derivation of that principle goes as follows. Let Alfred be our representative agent and dancing be our representative action. Suppose that Alfred is fully informed, that morality requires Alfred to dance, and yet that Alfred has no desire that would be served by his dancing. If, as we are supposing, morality requires Alfred to dance, then it follows from the Practicality Requirement that there is a reason for Alfred to dance. But if, as we are supposing, Alfred is fully informed, then if there is a reason for him to dance, he believes that there is a reason for him to dance. So Alfred believes that there is a reason for him to dance.

Now, the following modest form of internalism about reasons for action seems plausible:

> Reasons Internalism: If an agent believes that there is a reason for him to perform an action, and yet is in no way motivated to perform that action, then the agent is not fully rational.

The question of what marks an agent as fully rational is, of course, a difficult one. But the idea that at the very least, full rationality requires that one be moved to some extent by what one takes to be reasons is very plausible. A fully rational agent cannot be left entirely cold by what he takes to be a reason. (I will return in a moment to what happens if we deny Reasons Internalism.)

Now, I argued that Alfred believes that there is a reason for him to dance. Since we are also supposing that he has no desire that would be served by his dancing, it then follows from Reasons Internalism that either (i) Alfred is motivated to some extent to dance despite the fact that he has no desire that would be served by his dancing, or (ii) Alfred is not fully rational.

The first option, that Alfred is motivated to some extent to dance despite the fact that he has no desire that would be served by his dancing, is ruled out if we accept the Humean Theory of Motivation, which states that all "motivation has its source in the presence of a relevant desire and means-end belief" (Smith 1994, 92). The Humean Theory can be stated more precisely as follows:

> The Humean Theory of Motivation: An agent is motivated to perform an action if and only if he has some desire he believes would be served by his performing that action.

I think that the Humean Theory of Motivation is correct.[8] If it is correct, then Alfred's being motivated to dance implies that Alfred has some desire he believes would be served by his dancing. Now, because Alfred is fully informed, he will not *believe* that he has a desire that would be served by his dancing unless he really does have such a desire. So if Alfred is motivated to dance, then he really does have a desire that would be served by his dancing. But it was stipulated as part of the example that he has no such desire. Hence, he is not motivated to dance, even though he believes there is a reason for him to dance. We are, therefore, forced by Reasons Internalism to conclude that Alfred is not fully rational because he is not motivated to do what he believes there is a reason for him to do. In short, if Alfred is fully informed, and if morality requires Alfred to dance, and yet Alfred has no desire that would be served by his dancing, then Alfred is not fully rational. Generalizing, we have:

> Moral Internalism: If an agent is fully informed, is morally required to perform some action, and yet has no desire that would be served by his performing that action, then he is not fully rational.

4.4   Moral Internalism follows from the Practicality Requirement, Reasons Internalism, and the Humean Theory of Motivation. Within the context of the Practicality Argument for Agent Relativism, we can take the Practicality Requirement as given. Reasons Internalism and the Humean Theory of Motivation are then the only premises objectionable to someone who wanted to maintain the Practicality Argument. But these seem quite plausible.

With Moral Internalism in mind, I will now turn to Harman's argument against the claim that there is a universal moral requirement to refrain from killing innocent people. Harman claimed that Villain was fully informed, fully rational, and yet had no desire that would be served by refraining from killing his innocent victims. But if Villain really does not have any desire that would be served by his refraining from killing his innocent victims, then the Moral Universalist will respond to Harman's description of Villain by saying that Villain is either irrational—in that his desires do not reflect his beliefs about what he has reason to do—or that he is uninformed of the fact that there is a reason for him to refrain from the killings. In either case, according to the Moral Universalist, Villain fails to satisfy the conditions specified in the second premise of the Desire Argument, namely that the agent in question be fully informed, fully rational, and lack a desire of the relevant kind.

I should stress that I am not merely saying that because I have the intuition that Villain is morally required to refrain from killing his victims, I am therefore justified in rejecting Harman's intuition that Villain is fully rational and fully informed. Rather, my rejection is based on the fact that Moral Internalism is an independently plausible constraint that governs the desires of fully informed, fully rational agents. Our beliefs regarding whether or not Villain is fully rational depend upon our prior beliefs about his beliefs about reasons and about how his desires connect with those beliefs. Our judgment about whether or not Villain is fully rational is not a brute intuition, but rather is a judgment that we draw as a conclusion from our other beliefs about the way in which his desires match his beliefs about what there is reason for him to do. If Villain is stipulated to be fully informed, then our beliefs about whether he is fully rational will depend upon our prior beliefs about what reasons really exist for him to act in certain ways. In light of the Practicality Requirement, linking moral requirements with reasons for action, this means that our belief regarding whether or not Villain is fully rational will depend upon our prior beliefs about what morality requires of him. This is precisely the point at issue between the Moral Universalist and the Agent Relativist.

Thus, any attempt to provide support for the second premise of the Desire Argument by way of such examples begs the question against the Moral Universalist. In the absence of any other arguments, the Moral Universalist is free to reject the second premise, and along with it, the Desire Argument.

4.5   The previous argument relied on the principle that I called Reasons Internalism, which states that if an agent is fully rational and believes that there is a reason for him to do that thing, then he will be motivated to some extent to do that thing. A fully rational agent cannot be left totally cold by what he takes to be a reason. If Reasons Internalism is false, then the argument just given against the second premise of the Desire Argument is unsound. But—and here is the second horn of the dilemma—if Reasons Internalism is false, then the first premise of the Desire Argument is false as well, and so again, the Moral Universalist is free to reject the Desire Argument.

The first premise of the Desire Argument states that there is a reason for an agent to do a thing if and only if that agent would, were he fully rational and fully informed, have a desire that would be served by his doing that thing. But if Reasons Internalism is false, then that premise is false as well. If Reasons Internalism is false, then it is possible for a fully rational agent to believe that there is a reason for him to do something, and yet be unmotivated to do that thing. The fact that he is left totally cold by what he takes to be a reason does not mark him as less than fully rational. But now consider Villain. Harman asked us to suppose that Villain was fully rational, fully informed, and yet had no desires that would be satisfied by his refraining from killing his innocent victims. If the first premise of the Desire Argument were true, it would then follow that there is no reason for Villain to refrain from the killings. But if Reasons Internalism is false, it does *not* follow that there is no reason for Villain to refrain from the killings, for it may be that there is such a reason, but that reason simply fails to motivate Villain. It leaves him entirely cold. If he is not motivated in any way to refrain from the killings, then the Humean Theory of Motivation implies that Villain does not have any desire that he believes would be served by his refraining from the killings. Hence, either (i) Villain has no desire that would be served by his refraining from the killings, or (ii) he has such a desire, but does not believe that it would be served by his refraining from his killings. But if Villain is fully informed, and he has a desire that would be served by his refraining from the killings, he would believe that he had such a desire. So (ii) is ruled out. Hence, (i) Villain has no desire that would be served by his refraining from the killings, and the first premise of the Desire Argument is false.

4.6   So if Reasons Internalism is true, then the second premise of the Desire Argument begs the question against the Moral Universalist. If Reasons Internalism is false, then the first premise of the Desire Argument is false. Either way, the Moral Universalist is free to reject the Desire Argument.

5 THE NARROW DESIRE ARGUMENT FOR REASONS RELATIVISM

5.1   Can the Desire Argument be amended to avoid the objection raised in the previous section? I would like to consider an amended version of the Desire Argument that does not require that the agent be fully informed. Let us say that a fact is *a practical fact* if it is a fact to the effect that there is a reason for an agent to perform an action, or to the effect that there would be a reason for an agent to perform an action if a certain set of circumstances obtained. Examples of practical facts include the following:

- any fact to the effect that there is a reason for Jones to rake the leaves;
- any fact to the effect that there is a reason for Jones to not rake the leaves;
- any fact to the effect that there is a reason for Jones to rake the leaves in those circumstances in which his not raking the leaves would hurt his lawn;
- and any fact to the effect that there is a reason for Jones to rake the leaves in those circumstances in which he would enjoy raking the leaves.

The amendment, then, is to require that the agent be fully informed about all the relevant non-practical facts but to have no beliefs whatsoever about the practical facts. This yields the following argument for Reasons Relativism, which I will call the *Narrow Desire Argument*:

The Narrow Desire Argument

(P1) There is a reason for an agent to perform an action if and only if the agent would, were he fully rational and fully informed of all and only the non-practical facts, have some desire that would be served by his performing the action.

(P2) For any action, there is some agent who would, were he fully rational and fully informed of all and only the non-practical facts, have no desire that would be served by his performing the action.

(C) Hence, for any action, there is some agent for whom there is no reason to do that action.

Agent Relativism and Reasons for Action 45

I call this argument the Narrow Desire Argument because the range of beliefs it counts as relevant is narrower than the range of beliefs counted as relevant in the first Desire Argument.

5.2   What reasons are there for adopting the account of reasons for action expressed by (P1) of the Narrow Desire Argument? It has a number of aspects that need to be justified. First, what reason is there for excluding beliefs about the practical facts from our account of reasons for action? After all, the picture of a rational deliberator as canvassing what one takes to be the reasons for and against various courses of actions and forming desires and intentions in accordance with those reasons is very natural and attractive. But I think a relativist such as Harman would say that this picture ignores the reductive nature of his project. Harman is trying to give a naturalistically acceptable account of reasons for action, and he thinks, in line with the Humean tradition, that the only way to accomplish this is to reduce facts about reasons for action to facts about the desires one would have if one were fully rational and fully informed of all and only the non-practical facts. We exclude beliefs about the practical facts because our desires are supposed to be the source of our reasons, not the other way around.

That explains why the account of reasons for action expressed by (P1) excludes beliefs about the practical facts. However, there are other features that are in need of justification as well. The account of reasons for action expressed by (P1) is both agent-centered and desire-based. It is *agent-centered* in that it states that an agent's reasons for action are based only on facts about himself. It is *desire-based* because it states that the facts that are relevant are facts about the agent's own desires. Why does Harman think that giving a naturalistically acceptable account of reasons for action must commit us to this agent-centered, desire-based view? Harman says the following:

> Consider what it is for someone to have a sufficient reason to do something. Naturalism requires that this should be explained in terms congenial to science. We cannot simply treat this as irreducibly normative, saying, for example, that someone has a sufficient reason to do something if and only if he or she ought to do it. Now, presumably, someone has a sufficient reason to do something if and only if there is warranted reasoning that person could do which would lead him or her to decide to do that thing. A naturalist will suppose that a person with a sufficient reason to do something might fail to reason in this way to

such a decision only because of some sort of empirically discoverable failure, due to inattention, or lack of time, or failure to consider or appreciate certain arguments, or ignorance of certain available evidence, or an error in reasoning, or some sort of irrationality or unreasonableness, or weakness of will. If the person does not intend to do something and that is not because he or she has failed in some such empirically discoverable way to reason to a decision to do that thing, then, according to the naturalist, that person cannot have a sufficient reason to do that thing. (Harman 1984, 372)

Two different arguments are at work in this passage. They must be distinguished.

5.3   First, there is the argument that naturalistic scruples require that we analyze reasons for action in terms that are acceptable from a naturalistic perspective, or "congenial to science" in Harman's terms. Harman says that we cannot simply treat someone's having a sufficient reason to do something as irreducibly normative, and he says that this rules out our merely saying that someone has a sufficient reason to do something if and only if he or she ought to do it. The phrase on the right hand side of the analysis, "he or she ought to do it," itself needs to be explained from a naturalistic perspective.

I agree with Harman that we should not accept this as an analysis of reasons for action. But this does not require accepting an agent-centered, desire-based theory of reasons. After all, consider a theory of reasons for action similar to the one adopted by Thomas Nagel in *The Possibility of Altruism* (Nagel 1970).[9] According to this theory, the fact that an action would serve to satisfy someone's desire is a reason for everyone to enable, promote, or perform that action, even those people who themselves have no desires that would be served by serving other people's desires. From a naturalistic point of view, facts about whether or not someone's desires will be served by the performance of some action are perfectly respectable facts. Yet this is not an agent-centered theory of reasons for action. Therefore, the fact that we must analyze reasons for action in terms of facts that are themselves acceptable from a naturalistic perspective does not, by itself, require the agent-centered aspect of his theory.

Nor does it require analyzing reasons for action in terms of desires, either the agent's desires or anyone else's. There are a host of naturalistically acceptable facts that have nothing to do with desires but that are, nonethe-

Agent Relativism and Reasons for Action 47

less, plausible candidates for facts which are reasons for agents to perform certain actions. Remember, a reason for an agent to perform an action is a fact that supports its being the case that the agent ought to perform the action. There seem to be lots of facts unconnected to the agent's desires that are nonetheless prime candidates for being facts that are relevant to what the agent ought to do. For example, the fact that Alfred gave Bert five dollars on the condition that he would pay it back seems to be a prime candidate for a fact that supports its being the case that Bert ought to give Alfred five dollars, and so seems to be a prime candidate for being *a reason* for Bert to give Alfred five dollars. And even though this is a perfectly respectable naturalistic fact, it is not about anyone's desires.

Therefore, the claim that we must analyze reasons for action in terms that are acceptable from a naturalistic perspective does not, by itself, establish Harman's agent-centered, desire-based theory of reasons for action.

5.4   The second argument at work in the passage hinges on the relation between reasons and motivation. Because I have been carrying out this discussion in terms of "a reason" and "motivation," whereas Harman's passage is stated in terms of "reasons" and "intentions," we will have to extrapolate a bit to see how Harman's point bears on our discussion. Harman says that if an agent has a sufficient reason to perform an action, and yet fails to intend to perform the action, then this must be due to some "empirically discoverable failure." His examples of empirically discoverable failures reveal, with one exception, that the agent must be fully rational and fully informed of all the non-practical facts. The one exception is weakness of will, but Harman should not have included this on his list. To exhibit weakness of will is to give in to a strong desire to do something despite believing that there are overriding reasons not to do so. But allowing the agent to have beliefs about what reasons there are, together with the condition that the agent be fully informed, is going to open up the Narrow Desire Argument to the objection I gave to the less restrictive Desire Argument. Setting weakness of will aside, then, what we seem to have is that there are overriding reasons for an agent to perform an action if and only if the agent would intend to perform the action were he fully rational and fully informed of all and only the non-practical facts. Now, if that is the correct account of there being *overriding* reasons for action, then it also seems plausible to give an account of there being *some* reason for action according to which there is a reason for an agent to perform an action if and only if the agent would be motivated to some extent to perform the action, were he fully rational, and fully informed of all and only the non-practical facts. That is, Harman would have us endorse the following claim:

> Strong Reasons Internalism: There is a reason for an agent to perform an action if and only if the agent would be motivated to some extent to perform it, were he fully rational and fully informed of all and only the non-practical facts.

I call this Strong Reasons Internalism because it ties motivation to the existence of reasons, even though the agent in question has no beliefs one way or the other about what reasons there are.

It is the requirement that we give a naturalistically acceptable account of the link between reasons and motivation, as provided by Strong Reasons Internalism, that provides Harman with grounds for focusing on facts about desires, and, more specifically, for focusing on facts about the agent's own desires. According to the Humean Theory of Motivation, an agent will be motivated to perform an action if and only if he has a desire that he believes will be served by his performance of the action. Facts about other people's desires, if the agent has no desire to help those people satisfy their desires, and facts about the agent irrelevant to the satisfaction of his or her desires do not have this same tight link to the agent's motivation. An agent who is fully informed about what actions will actually serve his desires will be motivated to perform an action if and only if he actually has a desire that will be served by his performing that action. So, the Humean Theory of Motivation, together with Strong Reasons Internalism, yields (P1), that there is a reason for an agent to perform an action if and only if the agent would, were he fully rational and fully informed of all and only the non-practical facts, have some desire that would be served by his performing the action. Thus, Harman opts for the agent-centered, desire-based theory of reasons for action expressed in (P1) because he thinks it is the only way to give a naturalistically acceptable account of the tight link between motivation and reasons for action expressed in Strong Reasons Internalism.

5.5   But Strong Reasons Internalism is implausible. I agree with Harman that there is a link between reasons and motivation; as I mentioned, I find Reasons Internalism quite plausible. Recall that Reasons Internalism states that if an agent is fully rational and believes that there is a reason for him to perform some action, then he will be motivated to some extent to perform it. But the motivational link indicated by Reasons Internalism is mediated by the rational agent's belief about his reasons for action, and that is the key to its plausibility. Once this mediating belief is dropped, as it is in Strong Reasons Internalism, it is no longer plausible to suppose that an agent who is fully rational and informed of all and only the non-practical facts, will always be motivated to do what there is a reason for him to do. This is because a reason for an agent to perform an action is a fact that supports its being the case that the agent ought to perform the action, and it seems very plausible to suppose that there are facts that are relevant to what an agent ought to do that do not correspond in the required way with that agent's desires. When the agent reflects on such a fact, he may fail to be motivated by it because it lacks the proper connection with his desires, not because it is not a reason. To return to the example in which Alfred gave Bert five dollars on the condition that he would pay it back, would we even expect that condition of his promise to motivate Bert to repay the five dollars if we at the same time assume that Bert has no desires that would be served by his doing so? We can suppose that Bert has no desire to pay the money back, nor does Bert desire anything else from Alfred that he will not get if Alfred is mad at him for not paying the money back, nor does he have a desire to do what morality requires of him. It seems to me that if Bert lacks all those desires, then Bert would not be motivated to repay the money. Yet I see no reason for thinking that this lack of motivation on Bert's part undermines the claim that Bert promised is a fact that supports its being the case that Bert ought to repay the money. So Strong Reasons Internalism looks implausible when we examine its implications for particular cases.

5.6   It will be instructive here to look at John Mackie's discussion of the relationship between reasons and motivation (Mackie 1977, 27–42). In arguing for his error theory, Mackie says that if anyone were morally required to perform an action, then there would be "a reason for acting which was unconditional in the sense of not being contingent upon any present desire of the agent to whose satisfaction the recommended action would contribute as a means" (ibid., 39). But there could not be any such reason, Mackie says, for if there were, it would motivate the agent independently of any desire the agent has, and nothing motivates independently of desires (ibid., 40).[10] Hence, Mackie concludes, no one is morally required to do anything.

Harman agrees with Mackie in that he also thinks that motivation does not occur independently of desires, but he disagrees with Mackie in that he thinks that someone can be morally required to do something without there being a reason for acting which is unconditional upon the agent's desires: the existence of a reason based upon the agent's desires is enough. I think that Mackie is right: moral requirements are reasons for action that are unconditional upon the agent's desires. I also think that both Mackie and Harman are right that motivation does not occur independently of desires. But I think that both are wrong in thinking that there is a very tight connection between reasons for action and motivation. As Mackie himself observed, moral requirements seem to provide reasons for action that are independent of the agent's desires. It was only Mackie's implausible belief that such reasons would also *motivate* independently of the agent's desires that forced him to conclude what he himself granted was extremely counterintuitive, that there could not be any reasons for action that are independent of the agent's desires.

So, proper naturalistic scruples do not require an agent-centered, desire-based view of reasons for action, nor does the appropriate understanding of the relation between reasons for action and motivation require that we adopt Strong Reasons Internalism. Instead, it seems plausible to suppose that there is a class of naturalistically acceptable facts that are reasons for action, but which can be unconnected with the agent's desires.

5.7   In short, neither the Desire Argument nor the Narrow Desire Argument can be used in defense of Reasons Relativism. The Moral Universalist can plausibly claim to have an argument showing that either (i) any fully rational, fully informed agent would have a desire to do what morality required of him, or (ii) that it is possible for there to be a reason for a fully rational, fully informed agent to perform an action even if he would not have any desire that would be served by his performing that action. Either way, the Moral Universalist can reject the Desire Argument. Furthermore, the Narrow Desire Argument rested on an implausibly tight connection between the reasons there are for an agent to perform an action and the agent's motivations.

6 SUMMARY

6.1   When agents are subject to different moral requirements, this difference can be explained by their different circumstances and the application to both of them of some more qualified moral requirement that takes into account these different circumstances. This provides us with an argument for Moral Universalism. But if Moral Universalism is true, then we must find a response to the Practicality Argument. The first premise of the Practicality Argument was the Practicality Requirement, which states that if morality requires an agent to perform an action, then there is a reason for him to perform it. I argued that denying the Practicality Requirement is implausible. Therefore, we need to find grounds for rejecting the second premise of the Practicality Argument, Reasons Relativism. Reasons Relativism states that for any action, there is some agent for whom there is no reason to perform that action. The first argument for Reasons Relativism, the Desire Argument, either begged the question against the Moral Universalist or falsely supposed that any fully rational, fully informed agent will have a desire that would be served by his doing what there is reason for him to do. The second argument for Reasons Relativism, the Narrow Desire Argument, rested on an implausibly tight connection between an agent's reasons for action and the agent's motivation. In the absence of further argument, the Moral Universalist is free to reject Reasons Relativism, and with it, the Practicality Argument for Agent Relativism.

Chapter 3

Reasons for Action and the Ways of Being Good

1 THE PROJECT

1.1   It is a popular idea, and one that I think is correct, that one always ought to comply with one's moral requirements. Alternatively stated, it is a popular idea that there are always overriding reasons to comply with one's moral requirements.[1] Call this the *Authority of Morality:*

> The Authority of Morality: If morality requires A to ϕ, then there are overriding reasons for A to ϕ.

Perhaps *the* central question in metaethics is the question of whether the Authority of Morality is true, and if so, why it is true. In this chapter, I propose to set that question aside, and to focus on a more modest thesis, which I will call the *Relevance of Morality:*

> The Relevance of Morality: If morality requires A to ϕ, then there is a reason for A to ϕ.

The Relevance of Morality is more modest than the Authority of Morality in that it states only that there is *a* reason to comply with one's moral requirements, whereas the Authority of Morality states that there are *overriding* reasons to comply with one's moral requirements.

Is the Relevance of Morality true, and if so, why is it true? The Authority of Morality entails the Relevance of Morality, and because I think the Authority of Morality is true, I think the Relevance of Morality is true as well. But I will not argue for its truth here. Rather, I will take its truth for granted, and focus entirely on the question of *why* it is true. That is, although I will put the explanations I examine for the Relevance of Morality in the form of arguments with the Relevance of Morality as their conclusion, they would be considered blatantly question-begging if addressed to someone skeptical of the practical relevance of morality.

What accounts of morality and of reasons for action can we give such that even if they are not plausible to a moral skeptic, they are nonetheless plausible to friends of the Relevance of Morality and would explain why the Relevance of Morality is true?

1.2   It is important to note that the Relevance of Morality does *not* state that if morality requires an agent to do something, then that agent *has* a reason to do that thing. An agent may be unaware of a moral requirement, in which case he will not consider the fact that he has a moral requirement to be a reason. Alternatively, he may be aware of a moral requirement, but may deny that facts about moral requirements are relevant to what he ought to do. In this case, again, he will not take the fact that he has a moral requirement to be a reason. The Relevance of Morality is a thesis about what reasons *there are*, not about what reasons *agents have*.[2]

1.3   It is clear that on many accounts of reasons for action, the Relevance of Morality proves to be *false*. For example, many philosophers believe that the reasons for an agent to do something must be grounded in that agent's desires or interests. If an action would in no way further the agent's interests or the satisfaction of the agent's desires, then there is no reason for the agent to perform that action. Such views are inconsistent with the Relevance of Morality because it is possible for an agent to be morally required to do something that in no way furthers the agent's interests or the satisfaction of the agent's desires.

If the reasons for an agent to do something are not grounded in that agent's interests or desires, what are they grounded in? From what else could reasons for action arise, and arise in a way that would provide a plausible explanation of the Relevance of Morality? One source of reasons for action that many people have found attractive is goodness. Facts to the effect that an action would be good or would promote the good seem to be relevant to what ought to be done. Further, since it is an attractive idea that morality is concerned with the good (an idea that is attractive even to those who are not consequentialists), a good-based theory of reasons for action seems to hold promise for providing a plausible explanation of the Relevance of Morality.

2 THE WAYS OF BEING GOOD

2.1   But what if there is no such thing as goodness? Alternatively stated, what if there is no such property as being good? G. E. Moore said there is such a property. Goodness, he said, is "that quality which we assert to belong to a thing, when we say that the thing is good" (Moore 1903, 61). He offered the following argument for the conclusion that there is such a property. Moore said that 'good conduct' is "a complex notion: all conduct is not good; for some is certainly bad and some may be indifferent. And on the other hand, other things, besides conduct, may be good; and if they are so, then, 'good' denotes some property, that is common to them and conduct" (Moore 1903, 54).

But the argument is unpersuasive. It is no better than the following argument we get by substituting "big" for "good" in Moore's argument. "The notion of a big person is a complex notion: all people are not big; for some are certainly small and some may be average. And on the other hand, other things, besides people, may be big; and if they are so, then, 'big' denotes some property, that is common to them and people." But it is now commonly acknowledged that words such as 'big' and 'tall' do not express properties. (I present one version of the standard argument for this conclusion below.) Rather, they express relationships to comparison classes. When someone says, "That is big," or "That is tall," there is always some comparison class K such that what the person asserts is that the thing referred to is big or is tall *for a K*.

When we say, "John's conduct was good," are we really saying of John's conduct that it has the property of being good? In fact, we are not. As a number of philosophers have argued, attention to our linguistic intuitions about how the word 'good' and its cognates function shows that 'good' does not express a property. And it would be an odd view indeed according to which there is a property of being good even though it was never expressed by the word 'good'.[3]

Peter Geach argued against Moore's view, stating that "there is no such thing as being just good or bad" (Geach 1956, 65) on the grounds that 'good' and 'bad' are "always attributive, not predicative, adjectives" (ibid., 64).[4] He defined these terms as follows: "[I]n a phrase 'an A B' ('A' being an adjective and 'B' being a noun) 'A' is a (logically) predicative adjective if the predication 'is an A B' splits up logically into a pair of predications 'is a B' and 'is A'; otherwise I shall say that 'A' is a (logically) attributive adjective" (ibid., 64). Consider 'big'. If 'big' were predicative, then 'Hubert is a big mouse' would be equivalent to 'Hubert is big' and 'Hubert is a mouse', and 'Hubert is a big animal' would be equivalent to 'Hubert is big' and 'Hubert is an animal'. It would then follow from the truth of 'Hubert is a big mouse and a mouse is an animal' that 'Hubert is a big animal' is also true. But of course that does not follow. So 'big' is attributive. Geach also gave the examples of 'small', 'forged', and 'putative'. 'Tall' would be another example.

Now consider 'good'. If 'good' were predicative, then 'Jane is a good dancer' would be equivalent to 'Jane is good' and 'Jane is a dancer', and 'Jane is a good person' would be equivalent to 'Jane is good' and 'Jane is a person'. It would then follow from the truth of 'Jane is a good dancer and Jane is a person' that 'Jane is a good person' is true as well. But of course that does not follow. Hence, 'good' is attributive.

There are two problems with Geach's argument. First, it ignores the possibility that an adjective might be attributive in some of its occurrences and predicative in others. So it does not follow from the fact that 'good' is attributive in 'Jane is a good dancer' that it is always attributive. W. D. Ross is one philosopher who noticed that some occurrences of 'good' were attributive, but maintained nonetheless that some occurrences of it were predicative (Ross 1930, 65).[5] He says we must distinguish "between (A) the adjunctive or attributive use of the word, as when we speak of a good runner or of a good poem, and (B) the predicative use of it, as when it is said that knowledge is good or that pleasure is good" (ibid., 65).

Second, even if 'good' is always an attributive adjective, it does not follow that there is no such property as being good. Consider Geach's example of 'forged'. Geach is certainly correct that 'X is a forged banknote' is not equivalent to 'X is forged' and 'X is a banknote'. Indeed, the truth of any sentence of the form 'X is a forged K' does not imply the truth of (the relevant instances of) both 'X is forged' and 'X is a K', for it never implies the truth of 'X is a K'. Hence, 'forged' is always an attributive adjective. But this is not because it does not follow that 'X is forged' is true; rather, it is because it does not follow that 'X is a K' is true. A forged banknote is not a banknote, but it is, nonetheless, a forgery. A forged Vermeer is not a Vermeer, but it, too, is a forgery. Without knowing whether something is a forged Vermeer, a forged Monet, or a forged Picasso, one can still know that it is a forgery. Moreover, if you are speaking with someone on the phone at the Metropolitan Museum of Art who says "We just found out that the Vermeer we received last week is a forgery," you can know perfectly well what that person is saying without knowing whether what was received was a painting or a drawing. What you know is that it, whatever it is, is a forgery; that is, that it is a reproduction created with the intent to deceive others about the original creator of the work.[6] But if 'forged' is always an attributive adjective even though there is such a thing as the property of being a forgery, then Geach's argument that there is no such property as being good is invalid.

Judith Thomson appeals to a slightly different set of linguistic intuitions to argue that there is no such thing as goodness. Her argument for this conclusion is straightforward: whenever anyone says "That's good" of something, we do not know what that person has said unless the context makes it clear in what way the thing referred to is being said to be good. But if there were such a thing as pure, unadulterated goodness, then we would not need to know the way in which the thing was being said to be good in order to understand what was being said, for what was being said might simply be that the thing referred to is *good* (Thomson 1997, 276). This contrasts with the case of 'forgery', where we do know what is being said even without knowing what kind of thing is being said to be a forgery, or whose work it is a forgery of.[7]

This argument strikes me as correct. It avoids the second problem I raised for Geach's argument. However, it is worth noticing that it is subject to a problem analogous to the first problem I raised for Geach's argument. It is certainly true that in some cases, we do not know what is being ascribed to a thing when someone says "That's good." Consider Paul Ziff's example of 'This corpse is good' (Ziff 1960, 211). Because the context does not make it clear the way in which the corpse is being said to be good, we are at a loss to understand what is said. Is it being said to be good for use in practicing dissection, for use in practicing embalming, for robbing from its grave, or what? But what justifies generalizing from such examples to the very broad conclusion that this is true in every case in which 'good' is used?

There are various theoretical arguments that would justify such a generalization. Perhaps the most prominent is that if there were such a property as being good, then the belief that something is good would motivate the believer independently of any desires the believer happened to have. But because beliefs can never motivate independently of desires, it follows that there is no such property as being good.[8] I prefer to sidestep the issues raised by this argument. In this particular case, the linguistic intuitions seem robust enough, and the theoretical argument problematic enough, that the intuitions warrant more confidence in the generalization than would an appeal to the theoretical argument. Therefore, I will take it as established for the remainder of the chapter that there is no such thing as goodness.

If there is no such thing as goodness, what are we ascribing to things when we say "That's good"? We are ascribing to things one of what Thomson calls "the ways of being good," or what Georg Henrick von Wright calls "the varieties of goodness" (von Wright 1963). (I will use Thomson's terminology.) A property F is a way of being good if and only if it is a property that can be ascribed to a thing by saying of it 'That's good' or 'That would be good' or 'He's good' or 'She's good' or some such phrase. The ways of being good include being good to eat, being good for Alfred, being good as Hamlet, being good for use in making cheesecake, being good with children, and being good at hanging wallpaper. Further, there are the ways of being aesthetically good (for example, being pretty and being graceful), and, of particular importance to us, the ways of being morally good (for example, being just, being honest, and being kind).

2.2   The terminology of "the ways of being good" is potentially misleading in several ways. It is therefore worth guarding against a number of possible misinterpretations.

The first way the terminology can be misleading is that talking of the ways of being good suggests that there is such a thing as goodness itself. It is easy, then, to characterize the view as positing the ways of being good in *addition* to goodness itself, which is inaccurate. Michael Zimmerman, for example, characterizes the view using the following words: "if something is good, then it is good in some such way" (Zimmerman 1999, 395). But according to the view, that conditional is true, but vacuous, for if there is no such property as being good, then, *a fortiori*, nothing is good. Thomson herself sometimes expresses the view by saying that "a thing's being good just *is* its being good in this or that way" (Thomson 1992a, 149). But if there is no such property as being good, states of affairs that consist in a thing's being good do not exist, and thus are not identical with a thing's being good in this or that way. This mistake of thinking that goodness exists in addition to the ways of being good is understandable; normally, if there is such a thing as a way of being F, there is also such a thing as the property of being F. But in the case of 'good' there are only the ways of being good. The property of being good does not exist.

The normal relationship between being F and the ways of being F can be illustrated this way: consider that there are lots of ways to eat a Reese's Peanut Butter Cup, and there is also such a thing as the property of eating a Reese's Peanut Butter Cup. An agent has that property if and only if for some way of eating a Reese's Peanut Butter Cup, the agent is eating a Reese's Peanut Butter Cup in that way. So, Jones is eating a Reese's Peanut Butter Cup if and only if he is eating one quickly or slowly or normally, and so on for the rest of the ways in which one can eat a Reese's Peanut Butter Cup. But this situation, in which there are both the ways of eating a Reese's Peanut Butter Cup and the property of eating a Reese's Peanut Butter Cup, contrasts with goodness. As Thomson rightly points out, it is a mistake to define goodness as an existential generalization over the ways of being good (Thomson 1997, 277). She says that the property that a thing has if and only if it is good in some way or other is certainly not the property that friends of goodness mean to talk about when they speak of goodness. *Everything* is good in some way or other, but friends of goodness mean to be speaking of a property that it is possible for some things to lack. They intend to distinguish the actions that are good from those that are not, or the people that are good from those that are not, or the states of affairs that are good from those that are not. But if goodness were the property of being good in some way or other, there would be no such distinctions to be drawn. Even a person that the friends of goodness would say is bad is good for use as an example of someone not to emulate.

The second way in which the terminology of "the ways of being good" is potentially misleading emerges as follows. When one predicates 'is eating a Reese's Peanut Butter Cup' of someone, one does not say, for some way of eating it, that he is eating it in that way. If someone says "Jones is eating a Reese's Peanut Butter Cup," he has not said that Jones is eating it quickly, or eating it messily, or eating it slowly. What he has said leaves it entirely open in which way Jones is eating it. This is because all that the speaker said was that Jones is eating a Reese's Peanut Butter Cup. This contrasts, say, with the sentence 'Jones is tall'. Someone who says, "Jones is tall," *has* said, for some comparison class K, that Jones is tall for a K. If we do not know what comparison class the speaker had in mind, then we simply do not know exactly what the speaker has said. He may have said that Jones is tall for a basketball player, or tall for a jockey, or tall for a human being. In this respect, the ways of being good are like being tall, and are unlike being a way of eating a Reese's Peanut Butter Cup.

The third way in which the terminology is potentially misleading is illustrated by Geach's way of expressing the thesis that there is no such property as being good. Geach had expressed that thesis by saying "there is no such thing as being just good or bad" (Geach 1956, 65). But one might say that there is no such thing as being *just* a forgery, for nothing has the property of being a forgery without also having some further, more determinate property of, for example, being a forged Vermeer. This is compatible with its also being the case that there is such a property as being a forgery. So saying that there is no such thing as being *just* good is weaker than saying that there is no such property as being good.

2.3   What is it that all the ways of being good have in common, in virtue of which they are ways of being good? As Thomson says, "it is not just happenstance that the word 'good' appears in all of those expressions: its meaning surely does contribute to their meanings, and we need an answer to the question how it does" (Thomson 1997, 298). Commonness of meaning, of course, does not imply that there is one single property expressed by all the uses of the word 'good'. 'Tall' has the same meaning in all of its occurrences despite the fact that there is no such property as being tall.

One answer to this question has already been ruled out by the remarks in the previous section. It is not the case that what all the ways of being good have in common is that they are all more determinate instances of one, single property, viz., being good. So we should not think of the relationship between the ways of being good and the meaning of 'good' on a determinable/determinate model. At any rate, the model is inappropriate on grounds independent of whether or not there is such a property as being good. Crawford Elder offers a standard definition of a determinable property as a property that "can be possessed by a thing only by being possessed in one or another specific value or form, where the various possible values or forms are mutually incompatible" (Elder 1996, 150). But, first, the ways of being good are not mutually incompatible. A thing can be good for use in making cheesecake and good for use in making devil's food cake and good to look at. And, second, there are many things that are good in some way but that friends of goodness would not say are good simpliciter. For example, an evil person might be good for use as an example of someone not to emulate, but presumably would not be considered good simpliciter.

There are a number of other alternatives at this point. On some views, what is common to all the ways of being good is that they answer to *wants* in various ways. Thomson held this view in (Harman and Thomson 1996), where she said the following:

> Intuitively, the goodness of a thing must issue in some way or other from its answering to wants. (That it must is an intuition with a long history.) So in particular for the ways of being good: a thing's being good in this or that way must issue from its answering wants. That is plausibly viewable as what all the ways of being good have in common, namely that a thing's being good in each way issues from its answering to wants—its answering to wants in the relevant way, of course, for a thing's being good in way W might well be expected to issue from its answering to wants in a different way from the way in which a thing's being good in way W' does. (ibid., 133)

On other views, what is common to all the ways of being good is that they answer to *interests* in various ways. Ziff, for example, holds the view that "apart from certain minor, derivative, or deviant cases, 'good' in English means answering to certain interests," where the interests in question are determined by features of the sentence in which 'good' occurs and by features of the context in which the sentence is uttered (Ziff 1960, 247). Ziff draws our attention to the difference between the sentences 'That is a good corpse' and 'That is a good cadaver' (ibid., 211). Even though a cadaver is a corpse, the occurrence of the word 'cadaver' in the second sentence indicates that what is being said is that that is a corpse which answers to the interests that doctors have in dissection. But with respect to the first sentence, we are at a loss as to what is being said about the corpse because we do not know what interests the corpse is being said to answer to.

Ziff's view can clearly be expanded to cover goodness-for, since what is good for X can clearly be defined in terms of what is, on balance, in X's interests.

Some philosophers think that, in more or less complicated ways, interests reduce to wants. For example, Joel Feinberg says that "an interest, however the concept is finally to be analyzed, presupposes at least rudimentary cognitive equipment. Interests are compounded out of desires and aims, both of which presuppose something like belief, or cognitive awareness" (Feinberg 1974, 52). If interests reduce to wants, then views that unify the ways of being good in terms of interests need not be incompatible with views that unify the ways of being good in terms of wants.

But any view that attempts to provide a unifying account of the ways of being good in terms of wants runs into trouble. Consider the property of being good for my poinsettias.[9] Are there some wants such that being good for my poinsettias reduces to answering those wants? Whose wants would those be? Certainly not the wants of the poinsettias themselves. Wants are a kind of mental state, and plants have no mental states.

Perhaps the wants in question are my wants. After all, in most cases the owners or users of plants want plants that are in good condition, and hence, have wants that will be answered by doing what will be good for their plants. But this is not always true, and when it is not true, we will not be able to reduce what is good for the plants to what will answer to the wants of the plants' owners or users. Weeds provide the most telling example here. Since a weed is an unwanted plant, what is good for a weed will typically frustrate wants. Moreover, various kinds of weather and states of the soil were good for plants long before users or owners were ever on the scene.

The fact that an action can be good for my poinsettias even though it does not answer to their wants (for they have none) or to my wants does not entail that being good for plants does not reduce, in some more complicated way, to wants. For example, a third alternative would be that being good for my poinsettias reduces to certain of my counterfactual wants: wants I would have if I were different in some way from how I actually am. But the usual way of specifying the counterfactual wants in question would be to say that they would be the wants I would have if I were rational and fully informed. But, returning to the case of what is good for weeds, there would seem to be nothing incompatible with being rational and fully informed and yet having no wants that would be satisfied by caring for the weeds in one's yard. Indeed, quite the opposite.

A fourth alternative is to simply reject the idea that it is possible to do what is good for plants, and more generally, to reject the idea that it is possible to do what is good (or bad) for anything that does not have any wants and whose good is not reducible to the actual or counterfactual wants of others. This seems to be Feinberg's view. He says that although we do speak of conditions as being good or bad for plants, in this case, our way of speaking is simply mistaken (Feinberg 1974, 51). But this view is a non-starter. It is easy enough to specify what is good for a plant: something is good for a plant if and only if it is conducive to that plant's being healthy (Harman and Thomson 1996, 141–143). Given that it is clearly possible to do what will affect a plant's health positively or negatively, it is clearly possible to do what is good or bad for a plant.

A view that attempts to provide a unifying account of the ways of being good in terms of interests (and that does not reduce interests to wants) might be able to avoid these difficulties. According to such a view, what would be good for a plant is what would be conducive to satisfying its interests. Those interests could be spelled out in terms of health, or in terms of biological functions, or perhaps both.[10] Attributing health-based or function-based interests to plants would seem no more problematic than attributing health-based or function-based interests to *people*. Admittedly, a person's health is generally relevant to that person's satisfying his or her wants, but even if an action that improved a person's health did not in any way contribute to the satisfying of his or her wants, it would still be true that the action was, in some measure, in that person's interests.

It is not clear, though, that there is any advantage to using the concept of interests to provide a unifying account of the ways of being good. For it seems to be a tautology that what is good for someone or something is what is, on balance, in that person's or thing's interests. It does not seem any more informative to first reduce what is good for a plant to what is, on balance, in the plant's interests, and then to reduce those interests to the plant's health or biological functions, than it does to simply reduce what is good for a plant directly to the plant's health or biological functions.

So rather than taking the notion of interests as providing a unifying account of the ways of being good, it would seem to be more perspicuous to simply take goodness-for as providing a unifying account of the other ways of being good. Thomson explores the idea of unifying the ways of being good in terms of goodness-for (Thomson 1996). Unfortunately, I must leave these issues open.[11]

Let us return, then, to the question of providing a plausible account of the Relevance of Morality based on the ways in which an action can be good.

In Thomson's examination of the implications of this view—that there is no such thing as goodness, there are only the ways of being good—she argues for two theses: one about how the ways of being good relate to moral requirements, the other about how the ways of being good relate to reasons for action.[12] In this chapter, I will combine these two theses with an eye to investigating whether they provide a plausible explanation of the Relevance of Morality. I will argue that there is much to be said in favor of the two theses and of the explanation they provide of the Relevance of Morality. However, problems remain in the form of distinctions that, despite being intuitively plausible, remain in need of theoretically satisfying explanations.

3 THE WAYS OF BEING GOOD AND MORAL REQUIREMENTS

3.1 We want to know whether an account of reasons for action based on the ways in which an action can be good provides a plausible explanation of the Relevance of Morality. The first part of the project is to understand how the ways of being good relate to moral requirements. Thomson says that the relationship lies in the fact that morality requires avoiding actions that are morally bad in some way (Thomson 1997, 286). This needs explanation.

3.2 Thomson defines a virtue property as a property F such that there is a character trait consisting in a propensity to perform F-ish acts, and that character trait is a virtue. So being just is a virtue property because there is a property—being just—such that there is a character trait—justice—consisting in a propensity to perform just acts, and that character trait is a virtue. Being kind and being generous are also virtue properties. Being graceful, on the other hand, is not a virtue property because the character trait of being graceful is not a virtue.[13]

I will say that being just, being kind, being generous, and so on for the rest of the virtue properties, are *ways in which an action can be virtuous*. Further, I will say that an action is *virtuous* if, and only if, of the many ways of being virtuous, the action is virtuous in one of those ways. If an action is just, then the action is virtuous, and the way in which it is virtuous is that it is just.[14] I will say that being unjust, being cruel, being mean, and so on for the rest of the contraries of the virtue properties, are *ways in which an action can be vicious.*[15] And I will say that an action is *vicious* if, and only if, of the many ways of being vicious, the action is vicious in one of those ways. So if an action is unjust, then the action is vicious, and the way in which it is vicious is that it is unjust.

Thomson says that morality requires an agent to do something if and only if the agent's not doing that thing would be vicious in some way. Now, if W is a way in which an action can be vicious and if W is *also* a way of being bad, then I will say that W is *a way of being morally bad.* So if being unjust, which is a way in which an action can be vicious, is also a way of being bad, then being unjust is a way of being morally bad, and unjust actions are morally bad in that way. Analogously, if W is a way in which an action can be virtuous and if W is also a way of being good, then I will say that W *is a way of being morally good.* So if being just, which is a way in which an action can be virtuous, is also a way of being good, then being just is a way of being morally good, and just actions are morally good in that way.

Why distinguish between the ways in which an action can be virtuous or vicious and the ways in which an action can be morally good or morally bad? Because some philosophers would say that some of the ways an action can be virtuous are not also ways of being good, and so are not ways of being morally good. Also, some philosophers would say that some of the ways an action can be vicious are not also ways of being bad, and so are not ways of being morally bad. For example, some philosophers would say that being chaste is a way of being virtuous, but it is not a way of being good, and therefore is not a way of being morally good. They would say that being chaste is an aspect of morality that is old-fashioned, obsolete, or out-of-date, but is nonetheless still an aspect of *morality*. I am not suggesting that such people are correct in saying such things; indeed, they seem to me to be obviously mistaken. My point here is only that this sort of view is not ruled out by definition. It is a substantive claim that the ways of being virtuous are also ways of being good, and that the ways of being vicious are also ways of being bad.

So morality requires an agent to do something if and only if the agent's not doing that thing would be vicious in some way or other. But, Thomson says, the ways of being vicious are also ways of being bad, and so morality requires an agent to do something if and only if, of the many ways of being morally bad, the agent's not doing that thing would be bad in one of those ways. For the purposes of providing an explanation of the Relevance of Morality, we only need the weaker claim that if morality requires an agent to do something, then, of the many ways of being morally bad, the agent's not doing that thing would be bad in one of those ways. Of course, if the agent's not doing that thing would be bad in one of those ways, then it is a *fact* that the agent's not doing that thing would be bad in one of those ways. Hence, if morality requires an agent to do a thing, then for some way of being morally bad, it is a fact that the agent's not doing that thing would be bad in that way. I will call this the *Moral Requirements Thesis:*

> The Moral Requirements Thesis: If morality requires A to φ, then for some way of being morally bad, it is a fact that A's not φ-ing would be bad in that way.

The Moral Requirements Thesis tells us how moral requirements are related to the ways in which an action can be bad. I will now turn to the second part of the project: understanding how the ways in which an action can be bad relate to reasons for action. I will begin with Thomson's view from (Thomson 1999).

4 THE WAYS OF BEING GOOD AND REASONS FOR ACTION

4.1   Thomson says that the ways of being good relate to reasons for action in the following way: a fact F is a reason for an agent to perform an action if and only if, for some way of being good, F is the fact that the action would be good in that way (ibid., 13).[16] Call this the *Reasons for Action Thesis:*

> The Reasons for Action Thesis: A fact F is a reason for A to φ if and only if, for some way of being good, F is the fact that A's φ-ing would be good in that way.

For example, if Jones's taking a certain medicine would be good for him, then according to the Reasons for Action Thesis, the fact that his taking the medicine would be good for him is a reason for him to take the medicine. Or, if Jones's taking a certain medicine would be good for Smith (Smith is somehow relying on Jones's feeling well), then according to the Reasons for Action Thesis, the fact that Jones's taking the medicine would be good for Smith is again a reason for Jones to take the medicine.

I will now argue for two preliminary amendments to the Reasons for Action Thesis that I think leave the overall spirit of the Reasons for Action Thesis intact.

4.2   First, it seems intuitively plausible to think that if F is, for some way of being *bad*, the fact that A's *not* ϕ-ing would be bad in that way, then F is a reason for A to ϕ. But according to the Reasons for Action Thesis, F is not a reason for A to ϕ because F is a fact about the way in which A's ϕ-ing would be *bad*, not *good*. It might be tempting to avoid this complication by supposing that the fact that A's ϕ-ing would be good in way W is necessarily coextensive with the fact that A's not ϕ-ing would be bad in the way that is the contrary of W, and if those facts are necessarily coextensive, we might as well identify them. On this supposition, if A's not ϕ-ing would be unjust, then the fact that A's not ϕ-ing would be unjust is identical to the fact that A's ϕ-ing would be just, and so *would* be a reason for A to ϕ by the Reasons for Action Thesis.

But the fact that A's ϕ-ing would be good in way W is not necessarily coextensive with the fact that A's not ϕ-ing would be bad in the way that is the contrary of W. Suppose that Smith's taking a certain medicine would be good for him because it would cure his illness. Does it follow that Smith's not taking that medicine would be bad for him? Not necessarily, because Smith might instead simply take a different medicine that would also cure his illness. Similarly, it may be that Smith's giving a five dollar bill to Jones would be just, even though his not giving the five dollar bill to Jones would not be unjust, say, if he instead gave Jones five one dollar bills. But if the requisite facts are not necessarily coextensive, then they are not identical to each other. Thus, we cannot avoid adding a clause about the ways of being bad to the Reasons for Action Thesis.

4.3   The second way in which the Reasons for Action Thesis needs to be amended emerges as follows.

Suppose that Jones's taking a certain medicine would cure his sickness, and would therefore be good for him. According to the Reasons for Action Thesis, the fact that Jones's taking the medicine would cure his sickness is not itself a reason for him to do so, for it is not itself the fact that Jones's taking the medicine would be good for him. (His taking the medicine could be good for him even if, for example, it only alleviated the unpleasant symptoms of his sickness without actually curing it.) Thomson would say that it is at best a reason to believe that Jones's taking the medicine would be good in some way (Thomson 1999, 13). I think this aspect of the Reasons for Action Thesis should be rejected.

The fact that Jones's taking the medicine would cure his sickness is not merely a reason to believe that Jones's taking the medicine would be good for him; it is part of the explanation why his taking the medicine would be good for him. His taking the medicine would be good for him because it would cure his sickness, and *that* would be good for him. The fact that Jones's taking the medicine would cure his sickness contrasts with a fact such as the fact that his friend advised him to take the medicine. The fact that Jones's friend advised him to take the medicine *is* merely a reason to believe that his taking the medicine would be good for him. It is not part of the explanation why his taking the medicine would be good for him (although it would be part of the explanation why he took the medicine if he took it because his friend advised him to do so). And I think, intuitively, the fact that his friend advised him to take the medicine is not itself a reason for Jones to take the medicine. Jones's friend could advise Jones to do something that there is no reason for Jones to do.

Why count facts that are part of the explanation of why an action would be good in some way as reasons for the action? There are two reasons. First, doing so corresponds more accurately with ordinary usage. If we ask Jones why he should take the medicine, he might respond by saying that his taking the medicine would be good for him, but he might also respond by saying that his taking the medicine would cure his sickness. Indeed, I think it more likely that he would respond in this second way. It is more informative. There seems to be nothing odd or out of the ordinary in his doing so.

Second, a reason for an agent to do something is a fact that is favorably relevant to its being the case that he ought to do that thing. This definition requires that we allow facts that are part of the explanation of why an action would be good in some way to be reasons for action. Given the circumstances, the fact that Jones's taking the medicine would cure him is favorably relevant to its being the case that he ought to take it. Nonetheless, it is not identical to the fact that Jones's taking the medicine would be good for him.

4.4   We can still preserve the spirit of the Reasons for Action Thesis, though, by allowing that the fact that Jones's taking his medicine would cure his sickness is a reason for him to take his medicine *only if* that fact is part of the explanation of why his taking his medicine would be good in some way. Further, while the fact that Jones's taking the medicine would cure his sickness and the fact that Jones's taking the medicine would be good for him are two different facts, and so are two different reasons, they are not independent reasons: the first is derived from the second and adds no weight to the positive case for Jones's taking the medicine over and above the fact that his taking the medicine would be good for him. This contrasts with a case in which Jones's taking the medicine would be good for Jones (because it would cure his sickness), and would also be good for Smith (because Smith is somehow relying on Jones's feeling well).

Therefore, I think we should allow that a fact F can be a reason for A to φ even though F is not itself, for some way of being good, the fact that A's φ-ing would be good in that way. It is enough that it be part of the explanation why A's φ-ing would be good in that way.

Amending the Reasons for Actions Thesis to take into account these two points requires amending it to allow that a fact F is a reason for A to φ if, and only if, it meets any of the following conditions:

(i.a) For some way of being good, F is the fact that A's φ-ing would be good in that way.

(i.b) For some way of being bad, F is the fact that A's not φ-ing would be bad in that way.

(ii.a) For some way of being good, F is part of the explanation why A's φ-ing would be good in that way.

(ii.b) For some way of being bad, F is part of the explanation why A's not φ-ing would be bad in that way.

If a fact meets one of those conditions, I will say that it is "suitably related to some way in which A's φ-ing (A's not φ-ing) would be good (bad)." The Reasons for Action Thesis can now be stated as follows:

The Revised Reasons for Action Thesis: A fact F is a reason for A to φ if, and only if, F is suitably related to some way in which A's φ-ing (A's not φ-ing) would be good (bad).

5 THE QUICK ARGUMENT FOR THE RELEVANCE OF MORALITY

5.1   We have now in hand two interesting and *prima facie* plausible suggestions. First, we have the Moral Requirements Thesis:

> The Moral Requirements Thesis: If morality requires A to φ, then for some way of being morally bad, it is a fact that A's not φ-ing would be bad in that way.

Second, we have the Revised Reasons for Action Thesis:

> The Revised Reasons for Action Thesis: A fact F is a reason for A to φ if and only if F is suitably related to some way in which A's φ-ing (A's not φ-ing) would be good (bad).

Putting these two theses together provides a quick argument for the Relevance of Morality. Suppose that morality requires Jones to dance. Then by the Moral Requirements Thesis, for some way of being morally bad, it is a fact that Jones's not dancing would be bad in that way. But according to the Revised Reasons for Action Thesis (by clause (i.b)), that fact is itself a reason for Jones to dance. So there is a reason for Jones to do what morality requires. More generally, we have the following argument for the Relevance of Morality:

The Quick Argument for the Relevance of Morality

> (P1) If morality requires A to φ, then for some way of being morally bad, it is a fact that A's not φ-ing would be bad in that way. (The Moral Requirements Thesis)
>
> (P2) A fact F is a reason for A to φ if and only if F is suitably related to some way in which A's φ-ing (A's not φ-ing) would be good (bad). (The Revised Reasons for Action Thesis)
>
> (C) Hence, if morality requires A to φ, then there is a reason for A to φ.

What should we make of this argument? In section 6, I will indicate some of its attractions. I also think we should accept its first premise, the Moral Requirements Thesis, and I will defend that thesis against one objection in section 7. But I will argue that the argument's second premise, the

Revised Reasons for Action Thesis, is false, and hence, that the Quick Argument for the Relevance of Morality is unsound.

6 SOME ADVANTAGES OF THE QUICK ARGUMENT FOR THE RELEVANCE OF MORALITY

6.1   It will be worthwhile to briefly compare the Moral Requirements Thesis, the Revised Reasons for Action Thesis, and the explanation they provide for the Relevance of Morality with two other views. I think this will reveal some of its theoretical and intuitive advantages. It is an attractive view in many ways.

6.2   The first view attempts to base reasons for action on virtue, and has recently been defended by Gavin Lawrence (Lawrence 1995). Lawrence argues for a good-based account of reasons for action that states that it is conceptually true that there is a reason for A to φ if and only if A's φ-ing would be good. Therefore, it is true that there is a reason for A to φ if and only if A's φ-ing would be good. What is it for A's φ-ing to be good? Lawrence says that it is for A's φ-ing to be virtuous. It follows that if A's φ-ing would be virtuous, then there is a reason for A to φ.

There are three problems with Lawrence's account that the Quick Argument for the Relevance of Morality bypasses. First, Lawrence's account presupposes the existence of goodness, but, as I have argued, there is no such thing as goodness. The Revised Reasons for Action Thesis clearly avoids this problem by relying solely on the ways of being good.

Second, Lawrence's claim that for A's φ-ing to be good is for it to be virtuous is an excessively narrow understanding of the ways in which an action can be good, and it yields an excessively narrow account of reasons for action. An action can be good in some way without being virtuous; it could instead be graceful, or charming, for example. There could be a reason for Jones to tie his shoe, for example, even though in the circumstances, tying his shoe would not be virtuous in any way. Indeed, there could even be a reason for Jones to unjustly steal some money, for instance, the fact that doing so would enable him to buy some delicious lemonade. The Revised Reasons for Action Thesis allows for these possibilities because an action can be good in lots of ways even though it is not virtuous.

Third, Lawrence is mistaken in thinking that it is *conceptually* true that there is a reason for A to φ if and only if A's φ-ing would be good. Lawrence says that the fact that his account is conceptually true means that the "formal object of practical rationality" is doing that which would be good. Lawrence means that if A understands the fact that his ϕ-ing would be F to be a reason for him to ϕ, then, by his so understanding it, A thereby shows that he believes that his doing something F would be good. For example, suppose Jones is asked why he should give to charity, and he responds by sincerely saying that he should give to charity because his doing so would be kind. Then, according to Lawrence, Jones's responding in that way shows that he believes that his doing something kind would be good (Lawrence 1995, 130–132). According to Lawrence, then, the fact that his account is conceptually true implies that the only facts that someone can possibly take to be reasons for action are facts about what would be good.

The view that the "formal object of practical rationality" is doing that which would be good seems false to me. Suppose that Alfred has been persuaded by various philosophers that there is no such thing as goodness. But he does believe that there is such a thing as being good for someone, and so he opts for the popular idea that a fact F is a reason for A to ϕ if and only if F is suitably related to A's ϕ-ing (A's not ϕ-ing) being good (bad) *for A*. When Alfred deliberates about taking a trip to sunny Florida, he takes facts about whether it would be good for him to be reasons for action. He first tries to ascertain whether the trip would be good for him, and if he decides it would be, he concludes on that basis that there is a reason for him to take the trip. On the face of it, this seems to be a possible instance of practical reasoning. But, according to Lawrence, it is possible only if we can somehow find within Alfred the belief that his doing what would be good for him would be good. But Alfred sincerely and repeatedly refuses to admit this, for he does not believe in goodness. In light of his sincere and repeated disavowals, supposing that he has this belief seems implausible. Rather, it seems that he believes only that his taking the trip would be good for him, and that the fact that it would be good for him is a reason for him to take it.

If the formal object of practical rationality is not doing that which would be good, what is? Suppose that Jones is asked why he should give to charity, and he responds by sincerely saying that he should give to charity because his doing so is kind. What does that show about Jones's beliefs? Only that he thinks that the fact that his doing so is kind is *a reason for him to do so*. So I would make the rather banal suggestion that the formal object of practical rationality is doing that action for which there is a reason, not doing that action which would be good. More accurately, I think that the formal object of practical rationality is doing that action for which there are overriding reasons to do.

Whether or not this suggestion is correct, the Revised Reasons for Action Thesis is *not* a theory about what people take to be reasons; it is, as I said, a theory about what reasons exist. It is therefore compatible with the view that people can believe a fact to be a reason even if they do not believe it to be a fact about what would be good, and this third objection to Lawrence's account does not apply to it.

6.3   The second view attempts to base reasons for action on what is good for the agent who performs the action. Many people who might be attracted to an account of reasons for action based upon the ways of being good would nonetheless reject the Revised Reasons for Action Thesis because they prefer the popular idea I mentioned above, that a fact F is a reason for A to φ if and only if F is suitably related to A's φ-ing (A's not φ-ing) being good (bad) *for A*. According to this popular idea, the only way of being good that ever matters is the good-for way, and the only way of being good that matters regarding the reasons for a particular agent A is the good-for-A way. Such a view, however, has difficulties accommodating our intuitions about reasons for action. Facts about what would be good for others seem relevant to what an agent ought to do. Moreover, it might be that an action would be just even though it was not good for anyone. My returning Jones his cigarettes would be just (they are his, after all), and is compatible with its being the case that my doing so is not good for him, nor for anyone else. Nonetheless, the fact that the action would be just seems to be a reason to perform it. Such a view is clearly going to have difficulties accommodating the Relevance of Morality because it seems possible for morality to require an agent to do something that would not be good for that agent, but rather would be virtuous or good for some other person.

The Revised Reasons for Action Thesis bypasses these difficulties. According to it, the fact that A's φ-ing would be good for someone other than A is a fact that is suitably related to some way in which A's φ-ing would be good, and so is a reason for A to φ. Moreover, according to the Revised Reasons for Action Thesis, facts about the other ways in which an action would be good are also reasons to perform that action.

Here is an example that shows that the fact that an agent's action would be good for someone other than the agent is a reason for that agent to perform that action. Suppose that it would be good for Alfred if his sickness were cured. So anyone's action that would cure Alfred's sickness would be good for him, and so it would be good in some way. It then follows from the Revised Reasons for Action Thesis that there is a reason for any person, no matter who that person is or how that person is related to Alfred, to perform such an action. But does the fact that it would be good for Alfred if his sickness were cured really imply that there is a reason for, say, Queen Elizabeth to perform an action that would cure Alfred's sickness?[17] The defender of the popular idea would say no.

But, it seems to me that it does. Suppose that Queen Elizabeth needs to call one of her ministers. In order to do so, she has a choice of pushing a button on her left or a button on her right. If she pushes the button on her left, her minister will come. If she pushes the button on her right, her minister will come, and, miraculously, Alfred's sickness will be cured. Isn't there something to be said in favor of her pushing the button on her right? It seems to me that there is, namely, that her doing so would be good for Alfred. Suppose that the *only* difference between the queen's pushing the button on her left and the button on her right is that if she pushes the button on her right, Alfred's sickness will be cured, whereas if she pushes the button on her left, Alfred's sickness will not be cured. If that really is the only difference, it seems to me that, all things considered, the reasons that exist for Queen Elizabeth to push the button on her right override the reasons for her to push the button on her left. Alternatively stated, if that really is the only difference, she ought to push the button on her right, and so that difference is favorably relevant to its being the case that she ought to push the button on her right.

Thus, there is a reason for Queen Elizabeth to push the button on her right. What is *not* plausible to say is that Queen Elizabeth *has* the fact that her pushing the button on her right would be good for Alfred as a reason for her to push the button on her right.[18] Queen Elizabeth is, in all likelihood, unaware of the fact that her pushing the button on her right will be good for Alfred, and even if she were aware of that fact, she might not care one whit about Alfred. If so, then Queen Elizabeth will not take the fact that her pushing the button on her right will be good for Alfred to be a reason for her to do so, and she will have no such reason for pushing the button on her right. But that she has no such reason is consistent with there being such a reason, and so is consistent with the Revised Reasons for Action Thesis.

But how, it might still be asked, can a fact that might be totally unrelated to anything that the queen cares about be a reason *for her*? The answer is simply that what the queen cares about does not determine the ways in which an action *of hers* can be good.[19]

Thus, facts about what would be good for others do seem to be reasons, and because of that, I take it to be an advantage of the Revised Reasons for Action Thesis that it can accommodate that fact.

7 THE MORAL REQUIREMENTS THESIS

7.1 The explanation for the Relevance of Morality provided by the Quick Argument for the Relevance of Morality is an attractive one. I now turn to the premises of the argument itself. The first premise of the Quick Argument for the Relevance of Morality is the Moral Requirements Thesis. The Moral Requirements Thesis itself was the conclusion of a prior argument, which went as follows:

The Argument for the Moral Requirements Thesis

(P1) Morality requires A to φ if and only if, for some way of being vicious, A's not φ-ing would be vicious in that way.

(P2) The ways of being vicious are ways of being bad, and so are ways of being morally bad.

(C) Hence, if morality requires A to φ, then, for some way of being morally bad, it is a fact that A's not φ-ing would be bad in that way.

I think this argument is sound, and want to defend it against an objection to (P2). (P2) says that the ways of being vicious are also ways of being bad, and so are ways of being morally bad. As I mentioned, it is not true by definition that the ways of being vicious are also ways of being bad. The question then arises as to why (P2) is true. Well, for some property P, having the property P is a way of being bad if and only if having the contrary of P is a way of being good. Hence, the ways of being vicious are ways of being bad only if the ways of being virtuous are ways of being good. So: is it true that the ways of being virtuous are ways of being good?

Unfortunately, without an account of what marks something as a way of being good, no definitive answer is possible. Nonetheless, it will be useful to take a brief look at the example of kindness.

7.2   Is it true that being kind is a way of being good? Bruce Brower asks us to consider the following world, which he calls "W2":

> W2: As a matter of psychological fact, kind people become weak and powerless. They are indecisive, lose control of their lives, and become ineffective in relations with others. Only those who are not kind can become strong and take charge of their lives. They need not be cruel or vicious, but even isolated kind acts lead to the destruction of one's character. (Brower 1988, 679)

The conclusion Brower would have us draw about W2 is that "There is no reason for agents at W2 to act kindly" (ibid., 683), but the challenge W2 poses to (P2) is that some might be tempted to conclude that in W2, being kind is not a way of being good. I do not think that this is right, though, and offer the following argument for thinking that even in W2, being kind *is* a way of being good.

What would a world have to be like in order for it to be the case that in that world being kind is not a way of being good? It is not enough that in that world, there are further negative consequences to actions that are kind. It is highly implausible to think that an action that is good in some way can have no further negative consequences. I think that in order for a world to be such that being kind is not a way of being good, actions that are kind in that world would have to lack those features of kind actions that in our world make it the case that being kind is a way of being good. Clearly, what makes being kind a way of being good in our world is *not* that kind actions result in the agents who perform them being decisive, having control over their lives, and being effective in their relations with others. Thus, in W2, the fact that actions that are kind do not have those results leaves intact whatever features of being kind mark it as a way of being good. Thus, if being kind is a way of being good in our world, then it also is a way of being good in W2. Since it is plausible to think that being kind *is* a way of being good in our world, I conclude that being kind is a way of being good in W2 as well.

Can a stronger argument be made that it is *impossible* for an action to be kind if it lacks those features that in our world make it the case that being kind is a way of being good? If so, then we could establish not only that being kind is a way of being good in W2, but that being kind is a way of being good in any possible world. I leave this open.

It is worth noting that, even though in W2 being kind is still a way of being good, morality does not require an agent in W2 to perform kind actions; the cost to the agent is presumably too great. This is consistent with the first premise of the Argument for the Moral Requirements Thesis, which says only that morality requires agents to refrain from performing vicious actions. It does not say that they are required to perform virtuous ones.

Hence, the sort of possible world that Brower would have us consider is not a threat to either premise of the Argument for the Moral Requirements Thesis.

7.3   It is also worth noting that Brower's claim that there is no reason for agents in W2 to perform kind actions is mistaken. What is true in W2 is that if A's ϕ-ing would be kind, then A ought not ϕ. That is, even though A's ϕ-ing would be kind, there are nonetheless overriding reasons for A not to ϕ. But that is perfectly compatible with its being the case that there is a reason for A to ϕ; it is just that it is stipulated in the description of W2 that any action that would be kind would also "lead to the destruction of one's character." Surely any reason for an action provided by the fact that it would be kind is outweighed by the reason against that action provided by the fact that it would lead to the destruction of one's character.

So it is not true that in W2 agents ought to perform kind actions. Is it true in W2 that any fact to the effect that someone's action would be kind is a reason for that person to perform that action? It seems to be true. Even in W2, that an action would be kind is something to be said in favor of it. Thus, even in W2, the fact that the action would be kind is a reason to perform it. Not only do worlds like W2 fail to threaten the Moral Requirements Thesis, they also do not threaten the Revised Reasons for Action Thesis.

8 DIFFICULTIES FOR THE REVISED REASONS FOR ACTION THESIS

8.1   The second premise of the Quick Argument for the Relevance of Morality is the Revised Reasons for Action Thesis, which states that any fact that is suitably related to some way in which A's φ-ing (A's not φ-ing) would be good (bad) is a reason for A to φ. If it is false, then the Quick Argument is unsound. As I mentioned previously, I think that it is false.

We need to be careful, however, in determining why it is false. It is important to note that the Revised Reasons for Action Thesis only concerns facts about the ways in which an *action* can be good. It is not a thesis about the ways in which an *artifact* or a *person* can be good. There should be no question that facts about the ways in which an artifact or a person can be good are, at best, only tangentially related to reasons for action. For example, the fact that a knife would be good for use in cutting vegetables is a reason for action only in a restricted set of circumstances. If there is no reason for anyone to cut vegetables, or if there is only a reason for people to cut vegetables poorly, then the fact that a knife would be good for use in cutting vegetables is not a reason for anyone to use the knife.[20] Similarly, the fact that Jones is good at hanging wallpaper is only tangentially related to reasons for action. But because such examples do not concern the ways an action can be good, they do not pose any difficulties for the Revised Reasons for Action Thesis.

But is it true that any fact suitably related to some way in which an action, either A's φ-ing or A's not φ-ing, would be good or bad respectively is a reason for A to φ? Consider one implication of the Revised Reasons for Action Thesis:

>   (1) For any way of being good (bad), if F is the fact that A's φ-ing (A's not φ-ing) would be good (bad) in that way, then F is a reason for A to φ.

Now, (1) is true only if all the ways in which an action can be good are, as I shall put it, *necessarily normative*. A way W of being good is necessarily normative if and only if the following condition holds concerning it:

>   For any agent A and for any action φ, if F is the fact that A's φ-ing would be good in way W, then F is a reason for A to φ.

For example, no matter who the agent or what the action, if it is a fact that the agent's performing the action would be just, kind, or good for a person, then that fact appears to be a reason for the agent to perform that action. So being just, being kind, and being good for a person seem to be necessarily normative. Now, what (1) says is that *all* the ways in which an action can be good are necessarily normative, for what (1) says is that for *any* way in which an action can be good, if F is the fact that A's ϕ-ing would be good in that way, then F is a reason for A to ϕ. So (1) is true if and only if all the ways in which an action can be good are necessarily normative.

But it is not plausible to think that all the ways in which an action can be good are necessarily normative. For some of the ways of being good, it can be a fact that some agent's action would be good in one of those ways even though that fact is not a reason for that agent to perform that action.

For example, suppose that Jones's saving a certain apple core in the freezer would be good for use as an example of something that only an obsessive person would do. Being good for use as an example is a way of being good. Hence, it is a fact that Jones's saving the apple core in the freezer would be good in that way. But if there is no reason to give anyone an example of something that only an obsessive person would do, and there may well be no such reason, then the fact that Jones's putting the apple core in the freezer would be good in that way is not itself a reason for Jones to save the apple core in the freezer. Hence, this is a counterexample to (1).

A second counterexample: suppose that my singing Jailhouse Rock would be a good impersonation of Elvis. A good impersonation is an impersonation that is good in some way.[21] Hence, it is a fact that my singing Jailhouse Rock would be good in that way. But if there is no reason for me to impersonate Elvis, and there may well be no reason, then the fact that my singing Jailhouse Rock would be good in that way is not itself a reason for me to sing Jailhouse Rock.

A third counterexample: suppose that my waving my arms in a certain way would be good to look at. Being good to look at is a way of being good. Hence, it is a fact that my waving my arms in that way would be good in that way. But if there is no one around to see me waving my arms then there may well be no reason for me to wave my arms.

So being good as an example of something only an obsessive person would do, being good as an impersonation of Elvis, and being good to look at are all ways in which an action can be good that are not necessarily normative. They are thus counterexamples to the Revised Reasons for Action Thesis.

8.2   I mentioned that it is plausible to think that *being good for a person* is necessarily normative: for any agent A and any action ϕ, any fact to the effect that A's ϕ-ing would be good for a person is a reason for A to ϕ. But what about *being good for an artifact*? It does *not* seem plausible to think that being good for an artifact is necessarily normative. For example, my removing a certain rust spot from my lawnmower might be good for it, but if the lawnmower is going to sit in my garage and never be used by anyone again, then there may well be no reason for me to do what would be good for it. So in those circumstances, the fact that my removing the rust spot would be good for it is not itself a reason for me to remove the rust spot. Hence, this is another counterexample to (1).

As an even more vivid example, consider being good for a rubber band. My rubbing some rubber conditioner on a certain rubber band might prevent it from becoming brittle, and so might be good for it. But plainly, if no one is ever going to use that particular rubber band for anything, then there is no reason for me to do what would be good for it. So this is another counterexample to (1).

When is a fact that an action would be good for an artifact a reason for action? I suggest the following generalization:

> The Good for an Artifact Generalization: The fact that A's ϕ-ing would be good for an artifact is a reason for A to ϕ if and only if there is an antecedent reason for A to do what would be conducive to the artifact's being in a good condition.

The interesting thing to note about the Good for an Artifact Generalization is that analogous principles hold of other ways in which an action could affect an artifact. For example, the fact that Alfred's using the tray of his CD-ROM drive as a drink-holder would be *destabilizing* for his CD-ROM drive is a reason for him to use the tray as a drink-holder if and only if there is an antecedent reason for him to do what would be conducive to his CD-ROM drive's being in a *destabilized* condition. The fact that Alfred's using the tray of his CD-ROM drive as a drink-holder would be *bad* for his CD-ROM drive is a reason for him to use it as a drink-holder if and only if there is an antecedent reason for him to do what would be conducive

Reasons for Action and the Ways of Being Good

to his CD-ROM drive's being in a *bad* condition. But if the relationship between reasons for action and being good for an artifact is no different from the relationship between reasons for action and being destabilizing or being bad for an artifact, then being good for an artifact bears no interesting relationship to reasons for action.

8.3   There is no need to make an exhaustive examination of all of the ways of being good and their relations to reasons for action. The examples just given suffice to show that not all of the ways in which an action can be good are necessarily normative. Thus, the second premise of the Quick Argument for the Relevance of Morality—the Revised Reasons for Action Thesis—is false, and the argument is unsound.

9 The Revised Argument for the Relevance of Morality

9.1   But as I mentioned, it is intuitively plausible to think that some ways of being good are necessarily normative. What the above counterexamples show is only that not all the ways of being good are necessarily normative. They do not show that none of the ways of being good are necessarily normative.

We have been focusing on the ways of being good, but analogous principles can be constructed for the ways of being bad. I will say that a way W of being bad is necessarily normative if and only if the following condition holds concerning it:

> For any agent A and for any action φ, if F is the fact that A's not φ-ing would be bad in way W, then F is a reason for A to φ.

Examples analogous to the ones given in section 8 would show that not all of the ways in which an action can be bad are necessarily normative. But, again, some ways of being bad seem to be necessarily normative. For example, being bad for a person seems to be necessarily normative: for any agent A and for any action φ, if it is a fact that A's not φ-ing would be bad for a person, then that fact is a reason for A to φ.

If we could construct an account that distinguished the necessarily normative ways of being good or bad from the contingently normative ways of being good or bad, and further, if it could be shown that facts about the ways in which a vicious action would be bad are necessarily normative, then we would have a revised argument for the Relevance of Morality.

What differentiates the necessarily normative from the contingently normative? Further, why is it that any action that is vicious is bad in a way that is necessarily normative? Why couldn't we say, for example, that the fact that Alfred's not returning the money would be unjust is not a reason for him to return the money, even granting that being unjust is a way of being bad?

9.2   One story might go as follows. The reason why being good for a person is necessarily normative whereas being good for an artifact is only contingently normative presumably has something to do with a difference between people and artifacts. It would be no surprise if that difference were expressed by saying that people are *intrinsically valuable* whereas artifacts are not.[22]

Suppose it is true that people are intrinsically valuable, and that being good for something that is intrinsically valuable is necessarily normative. That is, if x is intrinsically valuable, then for any agent A and for any action ϕ, if it is a fact that A's ϕ-ing would be good for x, then that fact is a reason for A to ϕ. If a popular thesis about harmless wrongdoing were also true, then we would have a new argument for the Relevance of Morality that did not rely on the dubious supposition that all the ways in which an action can be good or bad are necessarily normative. The popular thesis I have in mind is simply that there is no harmless wrongdoing, by which I mean that any action that would be vicious would be bad for a person. The new argument would go as follows. People are intrinsically valuable. If people are intrinsically valuable, then the fact that an agent's action would be bad for a person is a reason for that agent to refrain from that action. Hence, the fact that an agent's action would be bad for a person *is* a reason for that agent to refrain from that action. But there is no harmless wrongdoing: if an action would be vicious, then that action would be bad for a person. Since the argument for the Moral Requirements Thesis says that morality requires an agent to do something if and only if the agent's not doing that thing would be vicious, it follows that if morality requires an agent to not do a thing, then the agent's doing that thing would be bad for a person. Since being bad for a person is being bad for something intrinsically valuable, it follows that if morality requires an agent to do something, there is a reason for that agent to do that thing.

This revised argument for the Relevance of Morality can be stated more formally as follows:

The Revised Argument for the Relevance of Morality

> (P1) People are intrinsically valuable.
>
> (P2) If people are intrinsically valuable, then being bad for a person is necessarily normative.
>
> (IC1) Hence, if it is a fact that A's not ϕ-ing would be bad for some person, then that fact is a reason for A to ϕ. (From P1 and P2)
>
> (P3) If morality requires A to ϕ, then A's not ϕ-ing would be vicious.
>
> (P4) If A's not ϕ-ing would be vicious, then it is a fact that A's not ϕ-ing would be bad for some person.
>
> (IC2) Hence, if morality requires A to ϕ, then it is a fact that A's not ϕ-ing would be bad for some person. (From P3 and P4)
>
> (C) Hence, if morality requires A to ϕ, then there is a reason for A to ϕ. (From IC1 and IC2)

10 DIFFICULTIES FOR THE REVISED ARGUMENT FOR THE RELEVANCE OF MORALITY

10.1 I think there are two problems with the Revised Argument for the Relevance of Morality. Let me begin with a problem for (P4). (P4) states that if A's not ϕ-ing would be vicious, then it is a fact that A's not ϕ-ing would be bad for some person.[23] As I mentioned, many people find this view plausible. Many people also find a stronger view plausible: that actions that are vicious are bad for someone other than the agent performing the action. Harm to oneself, on this view, is bad in some way, but it is not vicious. I have sympathy for the stronger view, but what causes trouble for it, and for (P4), are vicious paternalistic actions. My not giving Jones his cigarettes back when he asks for them might be good for Jones, and bad for no one else, but it might nonetheless be unjust because the cigarettes belong to Jones.

10.2 There is a second problem, which I think is more interesting.

According to the first premise of the Revised Argument for the Relevance of Morality, people are intrinsically valuable. But what is it to be intrinsically valuable?

Some philosophers would analyze intrinsic value in terms of reasons for action: roughly, an object x is intrinsically valuable if, and only if, the fact that A's ϕ-ing would be good for x or that A's not ϕ-ing would be bad for x are always reasons for A to ϕ. If we opt for this analysis of intrinsic value, then we have gone in a circle, for we were trying to use the claim that people are intrinsically valuable as an explanation of why being good for a person and being bad for a person are necessarily normative. That is, if we analyze intrinsic value in this way, then to say that people are intrinsically valuable is just to assert the claim requiring an explanation.

A second alternative, pursued by Zimmerman, is that intrinsic value is itself a way of being good (Zimmerman 1999). On this view, to say that something is intrinsically valuable is simply to ascribe a particular way of being good to that thing. The kind of goodness ascribed here, according to Zimmerman, is *ethical goodness*. Zimmerman goes on to tell us that to say that things are ethically good is to say that "there is a moral requirement to favor them (welcome them, admire them, take satisfaction in them, and so on) for their own sakes" (ibid., 405).

Zimmerman's use of the phrase "a moral requirement" is much too strong, though. Suppose, to take Zimmerman's examples, that pleasure, knowledge, and beauty are intrinsically valuable. It is far too strong to say that I violate a moral requirement if I fail to favor beautiful paintings. At most, the plausible thing to say here is that, other things being equal, I ought to favor beautiful paintings. In other words, the most plausible thing to say here is that if beauty has ethical goodness, then there is a reason for me to favor beautiful paintings. But if, to say that a thing is ethically good is just to say that there is a reason for me to favor it, then we have again gone in a circle. According to this view, to say that artifacts are not always intrinsically valuable is just to say that it is not always the case that there is a reason to do what is good for them. But this simply reasserts the very fact for which we were seeking an explanation; it does not explain it. Therefore, Zimmerman's account is no more helpful than the one that defines intrinsic value directly in terms of reasons.[24]

A third analysis of intrinsic value would be one according to which a thing is intrinsically valuable if and only if it is good solely in virtue of its intrinsic properties, independently of its relation to other things. Moore, for example, says, "to say that a kind of value is 'intrinsic' means merely that the question whether a thing possesses it, and in what degree it possesses it, depends solely on the intrinsic nature of the thing in question" (Moore 1922, 286), and the surrounding discussion makes it clear that the properties that determine "the intrinsic nature of a thing" contrast with a thing's relational properties. But this cannot be right, at least not as it stands, for if there is no such thing as goodness, then nothing is good, and, *a fortiori*, nothing is good solely in virtue of its intrinsic properties.

A fourth analysis of intrinsic value would be one according to which a thing is intrinsically valuable if and only if it is good, but not in virtue of its being useful as a means towards something else that is good. In short, a thing is intrinsically valuable if and only if it is non-instrumentally good. But, again, this will not do as it stands. If there is no such thing as goodness, then nothing is good, and, *a fortiori*, nothing is non-instrumentally good.[25]

I say "at least not as it stands" for the last two analyses, because it might be possible to modify them so that they are compatible with the idea that there is no such thing as goodness. We could modify the third analysis to state that a thing is intrinsically valuable in way W if and only if it is good in way W solely in virtue of its intrinsic properties. Indeed, this is suggested by the quotation from Moore, where he speaks of "a kind of value."

Turning to the fourth analysis, we could say that something is intrinsically valuable in way W if and only if it is good in way W, but not in virtue of its being useful as a means towards something else that is good in some way (either in way W or in some other way). Further, we could say that something is instrumentally valuable in way W if and only if it is good in way W in virtue of its being useful as a means towards something else that is good in some way. For example, we could say that Smith's taking his medicine is instrumentally good for him because it has effects, such as the relief of his disease, that are good for him. But the relief of his disease is non-instrumentally good for him. It would be good for him even if it turned out not to be useful as a means towards anything else that was good in some way.

Which kind of analysis is relevant for our purposes, the one that contrasts 'intrinsic' with 'relational' or the one that contrasts 'intrinsic' with 'instrumental'? For our purposes, the one that contrasts 'intrinsic' with 'instrumental' is relevant. Consider a nice example by Monroe Beardsley:

> A sheet of postage stamps has been misprinted—the central figure, say, is inverted. The stamps derive part of their value from their rarity. Is one of these stamps valuable, in part, for its own sake [that is, non-instrumentally]? Well, its value is not for the sake of anything else—if we speak of its philatelic value, not its market value. But is this value then intrinsic [that is, non-relational]? It seems strange to say this when it can be taken away, without altering the stamp at all, simply by having the Post Office Department print a few hundred million more copies. (Beardsley 1964, 1)

In this case, the rarity of the postage stamp, although a relational property, is nonetheless the source of a kind of non-instrumental value. Since we are in search of a source of a kind of value that itself gives rise to reasons for action, what concerns us is non-instrumental value, whether or not it is due to relational properties.

Can we then explain why being good for an artifact is not necessarily normative whereas being good for a person is necessarily normative by saying that whereas some artifacts are only instrumentally valuable in some way, all people are non-instrumentally valuable in some way?

The first question to ask is whether all people are non-instrumentally valuable in the same way, or are they non-instrumentally valuable in different ways? I expect that those who say that people are non-instrumentally valuable mean that they are all non-instrumentally valuable in the same way. What way is that?

Suppose that all people were just. A just person would not necessarily cease being just simply because he were to cease being useful as a means towards something else that is good in some way. So being just is a non-instrumental way of being good. But are all people just? Obviously not. Indeed, for any of the ways of being virtuous, it would seem implausible on its face to suppose that everyone is good in that way. Similarly for the ways in which a person could be aesthetically good, or good at an activity. Because I have not offered an exhaustive taxonomy of the ways of being good, or an account of the necessary and sufficient conditions for a property's being a way of being good, I have no general argument that there is no non-instrumental way of being good such that all people are good in that way. But it does seem implausible. At any rate, none of these seems plausible as an interpretation of what people mean when they say that people are intrinsically valuable.

How, then, are we to interpret the assertion that people are intrinsically valuable? I think we should interpret it simply as saying that there are always non-instrumental reasons for doing what is good for people. But then the claim that people are intrinsically valuable cannot itself be used to explain the claim that being good for a person is necessarily normative. Rather, it is merely a reflection of that claim.

10.3   The objection I brought against the Quick Argument for the Relevance of Morality was that the Revised Reasons for Action Thesis implied that all the ways of being good and all the ways of being bad are necessarily normative, and that this seemed manifestly implausible. Some ways of being good and some ways of being bad are only contingently normative. But all that we need to secure the Relevance of Morality is that the ways in which a vicious action is bad are necessarily normative. The Revised Argument for the Relevance of Morality tried to provide such an argument by claiming that people are intrinsically valuable, and that vicious actions are always bad for someone. But the argument foundered on the notion of intrinsic value, and it required denying that there could be wrongful paternalistic actions.

At this point, there are a number of possible responses. Perhaps all people *are* intrinsically good in some way. If so, then it needs to be established in what way all people are intrinsically good. Or, perhaps people are intrinsically valuable, even though they are not all intrinsically good in some way. If so, then intrinsic value cannot be defined in terms of being intrinsically good in some way, and some alternative definition of intrinsic value must be established. Or, perhaps the explanation of why being good for a person and being bad for a person are necessarily normative is not that people are intrinsically valuable. If so, then what is the difference between people and artifacts that establishes the case that being good for a person and being bad for a person are necessarily normative, whereas being good for an artifact is not?

I don't say these responses cannot be successful, only that I don't see how they will be.

11 SUMMARY AND CONCLUDING REMARKS

11.1   Morality is relevant to what an agent ought to do. Why? An account of reasons for action that is based on the ways of being good holds promise for explaining the Relevance of Morality in an attractive way.

The account sketched here—a fact is a reason for an agent to perform an action if and only if it is suitably related to some way in which the action would be good, or if it is suitably related to some way in which refraining from the action would be bad—is attractive in several ways. It provides an account of how there can be a reason for an agent to perform an action even though the action would not be good for that very agent. That is, it is enough that it be good for someone else. Moreover, the account is compatible with the fact that an agent can take something to be a reason for action without believing that the action would be good.

That account provided the premises for what I called the Quick Argument for the Relevance of Morality. If facts about the ways in which refraining from an action would be bad are reasons for performing that action, and if morality requires refraining from acts that are bad in some way, then there is always a reason for agents to comply with their moral requirements. But I argued that not all the ways in which an action can be bad are necessarily normative. So the Quick Argument for the Relevance of Morality was unsound.

I then explored one possible revision of that argument. If it could be established that being bad for a person is a way of being bad that is necessarily normative, and if it could be established that vicious actions are always bad for a person, then we would have an argument for the Relevance of Morality that bypasses the objection to the Quick Argument. But I noted that not all vicious actions are bad for a person, and I argued against using the notion of intrinsic value to establish that being bad for a person is a way of being bad that is necessarily normative.

11.2   Clearly, someone sympathetic to the account I have been exploring needs some explanation of the distinction between the ways of being good or bad that are necessarily normative and those that are only contingently normative. I argued against one possible explanation, but the idea that some ways of being good or bad are necessarily normative is very plausible even in the absence of an explanation of its truth. The problem is providing a plausible explanation of that idea.

Further, someone sympathetic to the account I have been exploring needs an account of what marks something as a way of being good. The idea that being kind is a way of being good is intuitively plausible, but even those who have no doubts regarding its truth should want to know *why* it is true. Further, there are skeptics about morality who claim that the ways in which an action can be virtuous are not ways of being good. Without an account of what marks something as a way of being good, the response to such skeptics must rely largely on intuitions that the skeptic claims not to share. Finally, there are hard cases that those who are not skeptics worry about. Is being chaste a way of being good? What about being humble? Some say they are, but some say they are not. An account of what marks something as a way of being good would help resolve these issues.

Afterword

Now that my reader has some familiarity with the arguments I present in this book, I would like to end by commenting on two final points: the general usefulness of Test and the difficulties in adequately defining Appraiser Relativism and Agent Relativism.

1 Test and Appraiser Relativism in Other Areas

I present and support Test in chapter 1, section 5. Test, you will recall, offers a method of assessing the reliability of a person's linguistic intuitions about the logical relations between assertions of incomplete sentences. As I mentioned in the introduction, the question of the extent to which our theories are constrained by people's intuitions is a contentious one.[1] Because Test applies to incomplete sentences generally, it can be used to help resolve disputes about appraiser relativism in areas other than ethics.

Willard Van Orman Quine, for example, argues that whether or not a sentence in a particular language is true solely in virtue of that language's semantical rules is a relative matter (Quine 1953). He says that 'semantical rule' is significant only if it is understood relative to an act of teaching someone the language in question. It is meaningless when taken to be an absolute relation between a rule and a language. Quine illustrates his point using an analogy with the notion of a postulate:

> Relative to a given set of postulates, it is easy to say what a postulate is: it is a member of the set. Relative to a given set of semantical rules, it is

equally easy to say what a semantical rule is. But given simply a notation, mathematical or otherwise, and indeed as thoroughly understood a notation as you please in point of the translations or truth conditions of its statements, who can say which of its true statements rank as postulates? Obviously the question is meaningless—as meaningless as asking which points in Ohio are starting points. Any finite (or effectively specifiable infinite) selection of statements (preferably true ones, perhaps) is as much a set of postulates as any other. The word 'postulate' is significant only relative to an act of inquiry; we apply the word to a set of statements just in so far as we happen, for the year or the moment, to be thinking of those statements in relation to the statements which can be reached from them by some set of transformations to which we have seen fit to direct our attention. Now the notion of a semantical rule is as sensible and meaningful as that of a postulate, if conceived of in a similarly relative spirit—relative, this time, to one or another particular enterprise of schooling unconversant persons in sufficient conditions for truth of statements of some natural or artificial language L. But from this point of view no one signalization of a subclass of the truths of L is intrinsically more a semantical rule than another. . . . (Quine 1953, 35)

Does Quine's view conflict with our linguistic intuitions? Suppose that Smith asserts, "The sentence 'All bachelors are unmarried' is true in virtue of the semantical rules of English," and Jones asserts, "It is not the case that the sentence 'All bachelors are unmarried' is true in virtue of the semantical rules of English." Intuitively, only one of them can be right. So Quine's view *does* conflict with our linguistic intuitions. Does that by itself show that it is false? Of course not, for those intuitions may be unreliable. How are we to decide which is right, Quine or our intuitions? Test provides a tool that can help resolve the issue.

Quine is also a relativist regarding meaning and reference. In "Ontological Relativity," Quine argues that there are expressions in other languages "that could be translated into English equally defensibly in either of two ways, unlike in meaning in English" (Quine 1969, 29). His most famous example is 'gavagai', which he argues can be translated into English equally defensibly either as 'rabbit' or as 'undetached rabbit part', if we make different adjustments elsewhere in our translations. Elaborating on what he means by "equally defensibly," he goes on to say that both translations would "accord perfectly not only with behavior actually observed, but with all dispositions to behavior on the part of all the speakers concerned. On these assumptions it would be forever impossible to know of one of these translations that it was the right one, and the other wrong" (ibid., 29). Rather than conclude that there is an eternally inaccessible, non-relative fact of the matter about what 'gavagai' means, Quine instead concludes that there simply is no such non-relative fact. Nonetheless, it is still true that 'gavagai' means 'rabbit' relative to one translation manual and 'undetached rabbit part' relative to another.

Suppose, then, that Smith asserts, "The expression 'gavagai' means 'rabbit' in English," and Jones asserts, "The expression 'gavagai' means 'undetached rabbit part' in English." Intuitively, only one of those can be right, given that 'rabbit' and 'undetached rabbit part' do not mean the same thing. How do we tell if that linguistic intuition is correct or not? Again, Test provides a tool to help answer that question.

There are other, more heady kinds of appraiser relativism as well. Some philosophers espouse appraiser relativism about truth and some espouse relativism about facts, saying that truth or facts are relative to a conceptual scheme or to a linguistic framework.[2] Unlike relativism about motion, which I argue is consistent with our linguistic intuitions, these more radical versions almost certainly conflict with many of our linguistic intuitions. Test can help us determine the weight we should give this fact in our assessment of those theories.

2 Defining Moral Relativism

It is notoriously difficult to adequately define moral relativism. In "Moral Relativism Defended," Gilbert Harman, perhaps the foremost moral relativist today, complains that non-relativists use what he calls a strategy of "dissuasive definition" through which "they define [moral relativism] as an inconsistent thesis" (Harman 1975, 3). And the most common response that relativists make to their critics seems to be that their criticisms arise from a misunderstanding of the relativists' view. These complaints are undoubtedly justified. However, the definitions that relativists have offered of their own views also leave much to be desired. Relativists must take part of the blame for their critics' misinterpretations.

For example, Harman defines one kind of relativism that I discuss in chapter 1 as follows:

> [M]oral judgments are implicitly relative to one or another morality in something like the way in which a judgment that someone is tall is implicitly relative to one or another comparison class. George can be tall in relation to one such class and not tall in relation to another. For example, George might be tall for a man but not tall for a basketball player. It makes no sense to ask whether George is tall, period, apart from one comparison class or another. (Harman 1978b, 146)

Harman's use of the term "judgment" is misleading. Strictly speaking, there is no judgment—or as I prefer to call it, proposition—that George is tall. The *sentence* 'George is tall' exists, of course, but the propositions that exist are that George is tall *for a man*, and that George is not tall *for a basketball player*, and so on. Otherwise, it would make perfect sense to ask whether George is tall, period, apart from one comparison class or another. One would simply be asking whether the proposition that George is tall is true. Analogously, then, on Harman's view there are no moral propositions. The moral *sentence* 'Lying is immoral' exists, of course, but the propositions that exist are that lying is immoral *relative to my morality*, and that lying is moral *relative to your morality*, and so on. The description of Appraiser Relativism that makes it appear as though there are moral propositions is part of the reason why some people find it to be incoherent. Propositions, by definition, have one and only one truth value, but the Appraiser Relativist appears to be saying that the moral proposition that lying is immoral can have one truth value relative to one morality and another truth value relative to another.

Moreover, Appraiser Relativists who surreptitiously pilfer the language of moral judgments disguise the fact that their view of the semantic and mental content expressed by moral sentences is at odds with the way we normally think about such things, as I argue in chapter 1. They deceptively make their views seem less counterintuitive than they really are.

Clearly, understanding the Appraiser Relativist's notion of an action's being moral or immoral relative to a morality is crucial to assessing the view, or even to understanding it. But this is not a locution that one normally finds in common usage. Thus, we need to be told how to understand it. What is a morality? The obvious answer would be that it is a set of moral propositions, but that cannot be right, for as we have just seen, the Appraiser Relativist thinks that there are no moral propositions. Harman tells us that they are "sets of values (standards, principles, etc.)," but he does not tell us what these are (Harman and Thomson 1996, 13). And even assuming we had an understanding of what a morality is, we would still need to know how to determine whether an action is moral or immoral relative to a morality. The obvious way to find this out would be to find out whether the morality implies that the action is moral or immoral. But, again, that cannot be the Appraiser Relativist's view, for two reasons. Moralities, since they are not sets of propositions, are not the kinds of things that can imply things. And the proposition that the action is moral or immoral does not exist. Thus, it is not implied by anything. Only propositions or sets of propositions can stand in implication relations. Moreover, since only propositions can be believed, it follows that people cannot believe in their moralities. What, then, is the relation between a person and his or her morality if not belief?

Finally, if a speaker asserts, "Lying is immoral," how does one determine which proposition the speaker expresses? In particular, how does one determine which morality figures in the proposition he expresses? Gleaning answers to these basic questions from the writings of Appraiser Relativists is extremely difficult. It is no wonder, then, that critics of Appraiser Relativism frequently get the details wrong.

It is also difficult to properly define Agent Relativism, the view I discuss in chapter 2. Jonathan Bennett defines this as the view that "any kind of action can be right in some possible circumstances" (Bennett 1995, 171). More precisely, for any kind of action, there are some possible circumstances in which an agent is morally permitted to perform an action of that kind. According to Moral Universalism (what Bennett calls "moral absolutism"), some kinds of actions are wrong no matter the circumstances. That is, there is at least one kind of action such that there are no possible circumstances in which an agent is morally permitted to perform an action of that kind.

But this way of distinguishing between Agent Relativism and Moral Universalism is not quite right. First, the distinction philosophers commonly make between *kinds* and *classes* (or sets) raises difficulties.[3] The distinction can be illustrated as follows. Suppose I have in my pocket a pen, a dime, some lint, and a paper clip. Although the objects in my pocket form a class, they are not all the same kind of object. There is no single kind to which they all belong. If one were to ask about one of the objects in my pocket, "What kind of thing is it?" it would not make any sense to answer by saying that it is an object in my pocket. That does not tell you what kind of thing it is.

The apples on a tree, however, are all of the same kind. If one were to ask about one of the apples on a tree, "What kind of thing is it?" one could properly respond by saying it is an apple. Kinds, it is said, "cut nature at the joints," grouping things together which have the same nature. Classes, however, can be groups of miscellaneous things with nothing in common.

With the distinction between kinds and classes in mind, imagine someone who believes, among other things, that one is always morally required to do God's will, no matter the circumstances. It is consistent with the spirit of Moral Universalism for that person to also believe that, although the actions that God wills one to do form a class, they are not the same kind of action. God wills John to rake the leaves, and God wills Bill to perform heart surgery. Are raking the leaves and performing heart surgery the same kind of action so that there is a kind of action that both John and Bill are required to perform? Intuitively, the answer is no. The person who believes that one should always do God's will does not, or at least need not, believe that there is a *kind* of action—violating God's will—such that there are no possible circumstances in which morality permits an agent to perform an action of that kind. Rather, this person may believe only that there is a *class* of actions that consists of all and only those actions that violate God's will, such that morality does not permit agents to perform any actions in that class. Such a person should surely count as a Moral Universalist. Hence, for one to be a Moral Universalist it is not a necessary condition that one thinks there is a kind of action that is always wrong. In some cases, it is sufficient that one thinks there is a class of actions such that it is wrong to perform any action in that class.

On the other hand, for one to be a Moral Universalist, it is not *in general* sufficient that one thinks there is a class of actions such that it is wrong to perform any action in that class. Even an Agent Relativist would want to concede that there are examples of trivial or contrived classes that correspond to universal moral requirements. One can form a class out of any group of actions (even an empty group). Hence, one can form a class out of all and only the wrong actions. It follows straightaway that there is a class of actions such that it is wrong to perform any action in that class, for by definition, the class consisting of all and only the wrong actions has as its members only actions that are wrong to perform.

Put another way, no sensible Agent Relativist wants to deny that the moral requirement to refrain from performing wrong actions is universal.

Nor would any sensible Agent Relativist want to deny the existence of a slightly different kind of universal moral requirement, which can be illustrated as follows. Suppose that the Agent Relativist thinks that Bill would be acting wrongly by breaking his promise at a particular time. The Agent Relativist will allow that there is a class of actions which has as its sole member Bill's breaking his promise at that time, and he will allow that it is always wrong for anyone to perform an action of that class. Of course, this is just a long-winded way of saying that Bill's breaking his promise at that time was wrong. It has no implications whatsoever for the question of whether it is ever permissible for other people in different circumstances to break their promises. So the distinction between kinds and classes will not serve to help us distinguish between the Agent Relativist and the Moral Universalist.

The Agent Relativist is more charitably understood as denying, and the Moral Universalist as affirming, the existence of some *substantive* universal moral requirements. But apart from trivial examples like those just given, it is not clear which moral requirements should count as substantive and which should count as trivial. Some say that the moral requirement to refrain from murder is universal, but trivially so, because 'murder' simply means 'wrongful killing'. Others object that it would have been morally permissible to murder Hitler.

Because the Agent Relativist does not want his position to be falsified by the existence of trivial universal moral requirements, he needs an account of the trivial/substantive distinction in order to adequately define his theory. Similarly, of course, because the Moral Universalist does not want the truth of his position to follow merely from the existence of trivial universal moral requirements, he, too, needs an account of the trivial/substantive distinction. But how to spell out that distinction is not clear.

Even if we had in hand a way to spell out the trivial/substantive distinction, another problem remains. Consider the views of Bennett. He is an interesting example because he is both an Agent Relativist and a consequentialist. He thinks that the right action is necessarily the one that brings about the best consequences. But, setting aside the concern that the actions that bring about the best consequences are not all of the same kind, it follows from Agent Relativism that in some possible circumstances it is permissible to fail to bring about the best consequences. If that is so, then those circumstances provide a counterexample to consequentialism.

Bennett avoids this inconsistency by stipulating that the kinds of actions to which Agent Relativism applies are not to be defined in terms of overall consequences (Bennett 1995, 165). He says, for example, "There is no absolutist/relativist dispute about the wrongness of φing where 'φ' stands for 'kill an innocent person when there is no good to be achieved, or bad to be lessened, by so doing'" (ibid., 165). Because consequentialism defines the kind of action it says is morally required as the one which brings about the best consequences, Agent Relativism, so qualified, is consistent with consequentialism.

G. E. M. Anscombe also seems to understand consequentialism as a kind of relativism, and Bennett cites her as someone who opposes Agent Relativism because she opposes consequentialism. Anscombe describes her own absolutist view as follows:

> it has been characteristic of [the Hebrew-Christian] ethic to teach that there are certain things forbidden whatever *consequences* threaten, such as, choosing to kill the innocent for any purpose, however good, vicarious punishment, treachery (by which I mean obtaining a man's confidence in a grave matter by promises of trustworthy friendship and then betraying him to his enemies), idolatry, sodomy, adultery, making a false profession of faith. (Anscombe 1958b, 35)

Are Bennett and Anscombe right in thinking that consequentialism is a relativistic theory? If they are, then the Agent Relativist should not be understood as denying that there are any universal, substantive moral requirements.

I think Bennett and Anscombe are mistaken in thinking that consequentialism is a relativistic theory. After all, if it were, it would put us in the position of having to say that a theory that states that there is a single, universal, absolute, fundamental moral principle from which all particular moral requirements flow is a relativistic theory. That certainly sounds implausible.

Further, if Bennett and Anscombe are correct, then the Agent Relativist should be understood only as denying that there are any universal, substantive moral requirements defined in terms of overall consequences. But then the position that contrasts with Agent Relativism is simply deontology, the idea that the right action is not necessarily the one with the best consequences. Surely the Agent Relativist's position amounts to more than

Afterword

an assertion of consequentialism, and surely the Moral Universalist's position amounts to more than an assertion of deontology.

Further still, saying that Bennett's consequentialism is relativistic while maintaining that Anscombe's view is absolutist requires that we find grounds for distinguishing between the two. Anscombe says that there is an absolute prohibition on killing the innocent. Bennett says that there is an absolute prohibition on failing to bring about the best consequences. Unlike the earlier trivial or gerrymandered examples of moral requirements that the Agent Relativist could concede were universal, consequentialism is definitely a substantive moral requirement. Why not conclude, then, that Bennett is just as much an absolutist as Anscombe?

One might point out that, according to Bennett, there is only one universal moral requirement, whereas, according to Anscombe, there are several. But surely the mere fact that Bennett's theory is more unified than Anscombe's does not provide us with grounds for thinking that Bennett's is more relativistic than Anscombe's. If anything, one would expect the opposite.

Further support for the claim that consequentialism should not be considered a relativistic theory is provided by the fact that the Practicality Argument for Agent Relativism would work just as well against consequentialism as it would against a view such as Anscombe's. According to the Practicality Argument, an agent is morally required to perform an action only if there is a reason for the agent to perform that action. But there is a reason for an agent to perform an action only if the agent would, were he fully rational and fully informed, have some desire that would be served by his performing that action. The argument continues: for any kind (class?) of action you like, there is an agent who would fail to have such a desire in those idealized circumstances. It follows that there is no reason for that agent to perform the action, that the agent is therefore not morally required to perform that action, and, finally, that the moral requirement is not universal.

In response to Anscombe's claim that one may never kill the innocent, the Agent Relativist would claim that there is an agent, whom I called "Villain" in chapter 2, who is fully informed and who has no desire that would be served by refraining from killing his innocent victims. There is nothing inherently irrational, the Agent Relativist would say, in Villain's deciding to go ahead and kill his innocent victims. It follows, according to the Agent Relativist, that there is no reason for Villain to refrain from killing his innocent victims, and that Villain is therefore not morally required to refrain from doing so. Hence, Anscombe is mistaken in thinking that the requirement to refrain from killing the innocent is universal.

Now compare what the Agent Relativist might say in response to consequentialism. Suppose that Smith is fully informed and deliberating about whether to transfer for free the deed of his house to Jones. Suppose that doing so will be quite costly to Smith, but will bring about a benefit for Jones that is slightly larger than the cost to Smith. Suppose further that the action would have no other consequences and that there is no other action open to Smith that would have better consequences. Consequentialism then implies that Smith is morally required to transfer the deed to Jones. If it is plausible to suppose that Villain would not necessarily be irrational in killing his innocent victims, it seems even more plausible to suppose that Smith would not necessarily be irrational in refusing to transfer the deed to Jones. But if the Practicality Argument for Agent Relativism would work just as well against consequentialism as it would against Anscombe's view, then I conclude that consequentialism is no more relativistic than Anscombe's view. Since Anscombe's view is clearly an absolutist view, we should conclude that consequentialism is as well.

It is worth noting, however, that there is one moral theory against which the Practicality Argument for Agent Relativism would not work, or at least it would not work given the plausible assumption that all fully rational agents desire to further their own interests. This would be a kind of ethical egoism, according to which one is morally required to do what is in one's interest, where one's interest is defined by the desires one would have, if one were fully rational and fully informed. Egoism, so understood, does posit a universal moral requirement, but the nature of that requirement would seem to be consistent with the Practicality Argument for Agent Relativism. So egoism, even though it is a substantive moral theory which posits a single universal moral requirement, could perhaps be considered a relativistic theory. To what extent the Practicality Argument for Agent Relativism actually supports egoism is a question I shall leave open.

Endnotes

NOTES TO THE INTRODUCTION

1. As I explain in chapter 1, by "asserted," I mean "uttered with assertoric force."

2. I expand on this point in the afterword.

NOTES TO CHAPTER 1

1. Two notes about my use of the terms "proposition," "sentence," and "assert" are in order. First, strictly speaking, it is propositions that are asserted, not sentences. Sentences are uttered with assertoric force. However, in this context, it does no harm to describe sentences that are uttered with assertoric force as being asserted, and I shall avail myself of this briefer locution. Second, I understand propositions in the usual way to be context-independent entities, and to be, strictly speaking, what is said or what is asserted.

2. James Dreier is clearly a Speaker Relativist (Dreier 1990, 9). Wong, I think, is also a Speaker Relativist (Wong 1984, 73).

3. In (Harman 1975), Harman clearly wants to allow that a person can use a moral sentence to make assertions about moralities other than his own. In (Harman and Thomson 1996), Harman does not explicitly say whether he thinks that the morality that figures in a person's assertion is always the speaker's own morality, but he does draw a close analogy between his metaethical view and the view that when someone asserts a sentence of the

form 'The mass of X is M', he thereby asserts the proposition that the mass of X is M in relation to the spatio-temporal framework that was "*conspicuous* to the person making the judgment" ([italics added] Harman and Thomson 1996, 4). The analogy suggests that on Harman's metaethical view the morality that figures in the proposition asserted will be the one conspicuous, or in my terminology, salient, to the person making the assertion. For a different interpretation, see Thomson's reply to Harman in (Harman and Thomson 1996).

4. Harman is clear on this point. He says that his view is about how we must understand moral sentences "for the purposes of assigning truth-conditions," and he emphasizes that his version of relativism "is no more a claim about what people mean by their moral judgments than relativism about mass is a claim about what people mean when they make judgments about mass" (Harman and Thomson 1996, 5).

5. Many relativists would not subscribe to this claim as stated on the grounds that some moral sentences are analytic. If a moral sentence is analytic, then its syntactic negation cannot be truly asserted and so, of course, both it and its syntactic negation cannot be truly asserted. Harman, for example, says that 'Murder is wrong' is analytic because 'murder' is simply defined as 'wrongful killing' (Harman and Thomson 1996, 9). But because my objections do not rely on such counterexamples, it will not be unfair to simplify the discussion by ignoring this complication.

6. David Kaplan has argued persuasively that any occurrence of 'I' always refers to the speaker, no matter what operators precede the occurrence in a sentence. It follows that the embedded occurrence of 'I' in (S3) refers to the speaker, even though it is preceded by the 'Bertrand believes that' operator. See (Kaplan 1977).

7. One further strategy warrants brief mention. Charles Stevenson claims that our intuition that the parties to moral disagreements cannot both be speaking truly is to be explained away as a conflation of two senses of disagreement, what he refers to as "differing in opinion" and "disagreeing in attitude." Two people differ in opinion if something that one believes is inconsistent with something that the other believes; two people disagree in attitude when they have opposed attitudes to something (Stevenson 1968, 82–83). For example, if I say "I want to go out tonight" and you say "I want to stay in tonight," we disagree in attitude even though we may not differ in opinion. But contrary to Stevenson's opinion, this is unhelpful in explaining

away our intuitions in the moral case. The fact that the two people in the example above disagree in attitude in no way undermines our clear intuition that the propositions they asserted are inconsistent; rather, they are obviously consistent, *despite* their disagreement in attitude. If anything, then, the example suggests that people's linguistic intuitions about when people differ in opinion are not easily confused by accompanying disagreements in attitude.

8. This useful terminology is from (Harman 1978), (Thomson 1992) and from Thomson's response to Harman in (Harman and Thomson 1996).

9. The idea that motion is relative is even granted by those such as Newton who believed in absolute space. Newton says that "motion and rest, as commonly conceived, are only relatively distinguished" (Newton 1966, 2). Absolute motion is simply motion, "as commonly conceived," relative to absolute space (Newton 1966, 7).

10. See 296b of *On the Heavens.*

11. It is also interesting to note that the center of mass of the earth-moon system is inside the earth's surface (Feynman 1995, 99), so we can understand why an assertion of "Essentially, then, the moon revolves around the earth" is true if we take the completing relatum to be the reference frame given by the center of mass of the earth-moon system.

NOTES TO CHAPTER 2

1. An agent is someone who is subject to at least one moral requirement.

2. Agent Relativism, so defined, is a version of what Lyons calls "agent relativism," in contrast to what he calls "appraiser relativism" (Lyons 1976). Whereas appraiser relativism addresses itself to features of the agent who is appraising the action in question, agent relativism addresses itself to features of the agent performing the action in question. As will become apparent, Agent Relativism is a version of agent relativism because it addresses itself to what desires the agent performing the action would have in certain idealized circumstances.

3. Because Moral Universalism purports to be a necessary truth, the existential quantifier that appears in its negation—Agent Relativism—should be understood as ranging over both actual and merely possible agents.

4. See (Thomson 1990, 12–15).

5. David Sobel discusses this point (Sobel 2001, 464–466).

6. Korsgaard's description of the skeptic is inaccurate, though. It may be

that once we see what is really behind morality, we will *in fact* cease to care about it, not because it is not something worth caring about but only because we are somehow confused or mistaken about the correct grounds for caring about something. What Korsgaard should have said is that the skeptic thinks that once we see what is really behind morality, we *shouldn't* care about it any more.

7. An agent is fully informed if and only if he possesses all the relevant information and does not possess any misinformation, has drawn all the relevant conclusions from that information, and has not drawn any mistaken conclusions from that information. The term "desire" should be understood broadly, including wants, longings, goals, etc. It is also worth noting here that (P1) does not say that there is a reason for an agent to perform an action if and only if he desires to perform it. There can be a reason for an agent to perform an action that he has no desire to perform (the action may be thoroughly unpleasant in and of itself). Nonetheless, according to (P1), there may be a reason for the agent to perform it, if doing so would serve some desire that the agent does have.

8. See (Smith 1987, 1988, 1994) for a full-fledged defense.

9. Nagel usually states his theory in terms of the promotion of interests, whereas I am stating a theory in terms of the satisfaction of desires.

10. Mackie's view is even stronger than Strong Reasons Internalism. According to Mackie, a fact that is a reason for an agent to perform an action motivates that agent to perform that action if he is aware of it, whereas Strong Reasons Internalism just says that it motivates him if he is aware of it *and* he is rational.

NOTES TO CHAPTER 3

1. See chapter 2, section 3.1 for more on the relationship between what one ought to do and what there are overriding reasons to do.

2. For more discussion of the concept of reasons for action, see chapter 2, section 3.1.

3. See (Geach 1956), (Ziff 1960), (von Wright 1963), (Williams 1972), (Foot 1985), (Thomson 1997), and (Thomson 1992a).

4. The idea that 'good' is attributive had also appeared in R. M. Hare's work (Hare 1952, 133).

5. Cited in (Thomson 1992a, 156).

6. Perhaps the intent to deceive does not have to accompany the act of reproduction. Consider, for example, the Italian sculptor Alceo Dossena who was an expert at reproducing ancient Greek, medieval, and Renaissance sculptures (Imbornoni 2002). Although he never intended to deceive anyone about the identity of the creator of his works, others came to believe the works were authentic and they were sold by people other than Dosenna under the pretense that they were authentic. Two of his relief sculptures are now kept in a gallery reserved for forgeries in the Victoria and Albert Museum in London. My own, not very firm, intuition is that Dossena was not a forger, but his paintings, once they were passed off by others as originals, were forgeries. At any rate, it seems clear that an intent to deceive at some point is necessary for a work to count as a forgery.

7. Thomson also argues that there is no such thing as being a good K, for some K. Rather, what is said when someone utters a sentence of the form 'X is a good K' is equivalent, for some way of being good, to the proposition that X is a K and X is good in that way. For example, what is said when someone utters 'This is a good book' is, in most contexts, equivalent to the proposition that this is a book and it is good to read. Or, what is said when someone utters 'Alice is a good person' may be equivalent to the proposition that Alice is a person and Alice is just. But if the context does not make it clear which way of being good the speaker means to be ascribing, then we simply do not know what the speaker is saying when they utter a sentence of the form 'X is a good K'. See (Thomson 1996, 277–278).

8. See J. L. Mackie's discussion of categorical imperatives in (Mackie 1977). This argument is common among emotivists as well.

9. See (Harman and Thompson 1996, 141–143).

10. See chapter 3 of (Varner 1998) for a helpful discussion of the notion of biological interests as it applies to both humans and plants. He argues that a sufficient condition for an individual A having an interest in X is that "X would fulfill some biological function of some organ or subsystem of A, where X is a biological function of S in A if and only if (a) X is a consequence of A's having S and (b) A has S because achieving X was adaptive for A's ancestors" (ibid., 68). Although Varner does not discuss the concept of health, I expect that an organism is healthy just to the extent that it is in a condition that is conducive to its satisfying its biological interests. If this is correct, there need be no incompatibility between understanding what is

good for a plant in terms of the plant's health and understanding it in terms of the plant's biological interests.

11. See (Harman and Thomson 1996, 131–147), (Thomson 1997), (von Wright 1963), and (Ziff 1960, 200–247) for further discussion of the interrelationships between the various ways of being good.

12. Thomson explains her view of the connection between the ways of being good and moral requirements in (Thomson 1997), and she explains her view of the connection between the ways of being good and reasons for action in (Thomson 1999). These have now been incorporated, with some revisions, into her book, *Goodness and Advice* (Thomson 2001).

13. It is worth noting that Thomson argues that the character trait of maximizing goodness-for is not a virtue, nor are courage, industriousness, or loyalty (Thomson 1997, 282–285).

14. Notice that unlike goodness, being virtuous is properly defined as an existential generalization over the ways in which an action can be virtuous. See (Harman and Thomson 1996, 185).

15. Notice that a virtue property and its contrary are not collectively exhaustive. My tying my shoe was neither kind nor cruel. Is it possible for an action to have both a virtue property and also the contrary of a virtue property? I am going to assume without argument that this is not possible.

16. Thomson actually says that a fact F is a reason for an agent to perform an action if and only if, for some way of being good, F is a fact "to the effect" that the action would be good in that way. For brevity, I omit the "to the effect" here and throughout the rest of the chapter.

17. Thomson raises this question (Thomson 1992b, 114).

18. See (Thomson 1992b, 111–112) for Thomson's observations on how the word 'reason' slithers between the reasons that there are for an agent and the reasons that an agent has.

19. See chapter 2 for my criticisms of the view that a fact cannot be a reason for A to φ unless it is related to something that A cares about because reasons for action must be related to what can motivate the agent.

20. See (Foot 1978c).

21. See (Thomson 1996, 277–278).

22. Are there things other than people that are intrinsically valuable? On some views, all sentient creatures are intrinsically valuable. On other views, all rational creatures are intrinsically valuable. On still other views, all life is intrinsically valuable. It would not surprise me if those who thought that

things belonging to a class C are intrinsically valuable also thought that facts to the effect that A's ϕ-ing would be good for something in class C were always reasons for A to ϕ. Further, it is plausible to think that some artifacts are intrinsically valuable. If so, then perhaps being good for such an artifact is a necessarily normative way of being good. But it is implausible to think that all artifacts are intrinsically valuable, and so it is implausible to think that being good for an artifact is itself a necessarily normative way of being good.

Another possibility, which I will not explore here, is to appeal to the concept of moral standing, and say that the difference lies in the fact that people have moral standing whereas artifacts do not. Suffice it to say, I think that appeals to the notion of moral standing will run into difficulties similar to the ones I raise for appeals to the notion of intrinsic value.

23. I should note here that (P4) does *not* say that if an action is immoral, then it is, *on balance, bad for people*. That would be objectionable to any non-consequentialist. An action can be unjust, and yet be, on balance, good for people. Dissecting Jones without his consent in order to distribute his organs to five people who need them to live might be, on balance, good for people (the good for the five might outweigh the bad for Jones), but it is still unjust, and hence, is still immoral.

24. Zimmerman mistakenly interprets Thomson as denying that intrinsic value can be defined as ethical goodness, or what Thomson refers to as moral goodness (Zimmerman 1999, 406–407). To the contrary, Thomson offers a definition of intrinsic value in terms of what there is reason for everyone to aim at that is very similar to Zimmerman's own definition (Thomson 1992, 108–114). The problem Thomson raises with such an analysis is simply that "defining intrinsic goodness in terms of the word 'ought' gets things backwards for the purposes of the contemporary philosopher who makes use of that notion" (ibid., 114). If one gives an account of what one ought to do in terms of intrinsic value and also defines intrinsic value in terms of what one ought to do, other things being equal, then the account of 'ought' is circular.

25. Ziff, having argued that 'good' has associated with it the condition of answering to certain interests, where the interests in question are indicated by the context or by the phrase modified by 'good', suggests the following understanding of intrinsic value. He says, "suppose ... that 'good' is modified in such a way that an element modified by 'good' in an utterance serves

to indicate the relevant interest by characterizing something that constitutes the satisfaction of that interest: one would then have an utterance concerned with what philosophers have spoken of as something 'intrinsically good'" (Ziff 1960, 238). So although 'cadaver' characterizes a corpse in a way that leaves it open whether or not the corpse will in fact answer to doctors' medical interests in dissection, a normatively loaded term such as 'charitable' in 'It is good to be charitable' does not leave it open. Ziff says, "Being charitable answers to the relevant interest and cannot fail to do so in that it itself constitutes the satisfaction of that interest, viz., an interest in being charitable" (ibid., 238). The interests in question, contrary to what Ziff says, are not the agent's interests in being charitable (charity, by definition, takes place at some cost to the agent who is charitable), but rather, the interests of the recipients of the charity. Nonetheless, Ziff is correct in saying that being charitable necessarily answers to the relevant interests: if an act which purports to be charitable does not in fact help its intended recipients, then it is not really an act of charity. Unfortunately, Ziff's analysis fails when it comes to such sentences as 'Healthy food is good'. Healthy food cannot fail to answer to the relevant interests, but on no account is healthy food *intrinsically* good.

NOTES TO THE AFTERWORD

1. I do not refer here to the question of the extent to which we should hold substantive moral theories captive to our *moral* intuitions. That question, too, is contentious, but what I refer to here is the question of the extent to which we should hold theories that are largely conceptual captive to our *linguistic* intuitions.

2. See, for example, (Carnap 1950), (Goodman 1978, 91–140), and (Putnam 1981).

3. See (Armstrong 1989) for arguments for why we must distinguish between kinds and classes.

Bibliography

Abell, George O. 1982. *Exploration of the universe*. 4th ed. Los Angeles: Saunders College Publishing.

Anscombe, G. E. M. 1958a. On brute facts. *Analysis* 18: 69–72.

———. 1958b. Modern moral philosophy. Reprinted in *Virtue ethics*, edited by Roger Crisp and Michael Slote. Oxford: Oxford University Press, 1998.

Aristotle. 1941. On the heavens. In *The basic works of Aristotle*. Edited by Richard McKeon. New York: Random House, Inc.

Armstrong, David. 1989. *Universals: An opinionated introduction*. Boulder: Westview Press.

Beardsley, Monroe. 1964. Intrinsic value. *Philosophy and Phenomenological Research* 26: 1–17.

Bennett, Jonathan. 1995. *The act itself*. Oxford: Oxford University Press.

Brink, David. 1997. Moral motivation. *Ethics* 108: 4–32.

Brower, Bruce W. 1988. Virtue concepts and ethical realism. *The Journal of Philosophy* 85: 675–693.

Carnap, Rudolf. 1950. Empiricism, semantics, and ontology. *Revue Internationale de Philosophie* 4: 20–40. Reprinted in *Meaning and necessity: A study in semantics and modal logic*, by Rudolf Carnap. Chicago: University of Chicago Press, 1956.

Dreier, James. 1990. Internalism and speaker relativism. *Ethics* 101: 6–26.

Einstein, Albert. 1961. *Relativity*. New York: Crown Publishers, Inc.

Elder, Crawford L. 1996. Realism and determinable properties. *Philosophy* and *Phenomenological Research* 56: 149–159.

Feinberg, Joel. 1974. The rights of animals and unborn generations. In *Philosophy and environmental crisis*, edited by William T. Blackstone. Athens: University of Georgia Press, 1974.

Feynman, Richard P. 1995. *Six easy pieces*. Reading, Massachusetts: Addison-Wesley Publishing Company.

Foot, Philippa. 1967. *Theories of ethics*. New York: Oxford University Press.

———. 1972. Morality as a system of hypothetical imperatives. Reprinted (with revisions) in (Foot 1978a).

———. 1978a. *Virtues and vices and other essays in moral philosophy*. Oxford: Basil Blackwell.

———. 1978b. Are moral considerations overriding? Reprinted in (Foot 1978a).

———. 1978c. Goodness and choice. Reprinted in (Foot 1978a).

———. 1978d. Virtues and vices. Reprinted in (Foot 1978a).

———. 1985. Utilitarianism and the virtues. *Mind* 94: 196–209.

Geach, Peter. 1956. Good and evil. Reprinted in (Foot 1967).

Goodman, Nelson. 1978. *Ways of worldmaking*. Indianapolis: Hackett Publishing Company, Inc.

Gowans, Christopher. 2000. Introduction: Debates about moral disagreements. In *Moral disagreements: Classical and contemporary readings*, edited by Christopher W. Gowans. New York: Routledge, 2000.

Harman, Gilbert. 1975. Moral relativism defended. *The Philosophical Review* 84: 3–22.

———. 1977. *The nature of morality: An introduction to ethics*. New York: Oxford University Press.

———. 1978a. Relativistic ethics: Morality as politics. In *Midwest studies in philosophy III: Studies in ethical theory*, edited by Peter A. French, Theodore E. Uehling, Jr., and Howard K. Wettstein. Minneapolis: University of Minnesota Press, 1978.

———. 1978b. What is moral relativism? In *Values and morals*, edited by A. I. Goldman and J. Kim. Dordrecth, Holland: D. Reidel Publishing Company.

———. 1984. Is there a single true morality? Reprinted in *Relativism: Interpretation and confrontation*, edited by Michael Krausz. Notre Dame, Indiana: University of Notre Dame Press, 1989.

Harman, Gilbert and Judith Jarvis Thomson. 1996. *Moral relativism and moral objectivity*, edited by E. Sosa, *Great debates in philosophy*. Cambridge, Massachusetts: Blackwell Publishers, Ltd.

Hoskins, Michael. 1997a. *Astronomy*. Cambridge, United Kingdom: Cambridge University Press.

———. 1997b. From geometry to physics: astronomy transformed. In (Hoskins 1997a).

———. 1997c. The astronomy of the universe of stars. In (Hoskins 1997a).

Hursthouse, Rosalind, Gavin Lawrence, and Warren Quinn. 1995. *Virtues and reasons: Philippa Foot and moral theory*. Oxford: Clarendon Press.

Imbornoni, Ann Marie. 2002. The art of deception. Available at http://www.infoplease.com/spot/hoax5.html.

Kaplan, David. 1977. Demonstratives: An essay on the semantics, logic, metaphysics, and epistemology of demonstratives and other indexicals. In *Themes from Kaplan*, edited by J. Almog, J. Perry, and H. Wettstein. Oxford: Oxford University Press, 1989.

Korsgaard, Christine. 1996. *The sources of normativity*. Cambridge, United Kingdom: The Press Syndicate of the University of Cambridge.

Lawrence, Gavin. 1995. The rationality of morality. In (Hursthouse, Lawrence, and Quinn 1995).

Lyons, David. 1976. Ethical relativism and the problem of incoherence. Reprinted in *Relativism: Cognitive and moral*, edited by J. W. Meiland and M. Krausz. Notre Dame, Indiana: University of Notre Dame Press, 1982.

Mackie, J. L. 1977. *Ethics: Inventing right and wrong*. London: Penguin Books.

Moore, G. E. 1903. *Principia ethica*, edited by Thomas Baldwin. Cambridge: Cambridge University Press, 1993.

———. 1922. The conception of intrinsic value. Reprinted in (Moore 1903).

Nagel, Thomas. 1970. *The possibility of altruism*. Princeton: Princeton University Press.

Newton, Isaac. 1966. *Principia*. 3rd ed. Berkeley and Los Angeles, California: University of California Press.

Plato. 1992. *Republic*. Translated by G. M. A. Grube, revised by C. D. C. Reeve. Indianapolis: Hackett Publishing Company, Inc.

Putnam, Hilary. 1981. *Reason, truth, and history*. Cambridge: Cambridge University Press.

Quine, Willard Van Orman. 1953. Two dogmas of empiricism. In *From a logical point of view*. Cambridge, Massachusetts: Harvard University Press.

———. 1969. Ontological relativity. Reprinted in *Ontological relativity and other essays*. New York: Columbia University Press, 1969.

Ross, David. 1930. *The right and the good*. Oxford: Oxford University Press.

Smith, Michael. 1987. The humean theory of motivation. *Mind* 96: 36–61.

———. 1988. On humeans, anti-humeans, and motivation: A reply to Petit. *Mind* 97: 589–595.

———. 1994. *The moral problem*. Oxford: Blackwell.

Sobel, David. 2001. Subjective accounts of reasons for action. *Ethics* 111: 461–492.

Stevenson, Charles L. 1968. Moore's arguments against certain forms of ethical naturalism. In *The philosophy of G. E. Moore*, edited by Paul Arthur Schilpp. La Salle, Illinois: Open Court, 1968.

Thomson, Judith Jarvis. 1983. Imposing risks. Reprinted in *Rights, restitution, and risk*, edited by William Parent. Cambridge, Massachusetts: Harvard University Press, 1986.

———. 1990. *The realm of rights*. Cambridge, Massachusetts: Harvard University Press.

———. 1992a. Goodness and utilitarianism. Paper read at the Eighty-Ninth Annual Eastern Division Meeting of the American Philosophical Association, at Washington, D. C.

———. 1992b. Some ways in which a thing can be good. *Social Philosophy and Policy* 9: 96–117.

———. 1997. The right and the good. *The Journal of Philosophy* 94: 273–298.

———. 1999. Desire and the good. Paper read at the 1999 Central Meeting of the American Philosophical Association, at New Orleans, Louisiana.

———. 2001. *Goodness and advice*, edited by Amy Gutmann. Princeton: Princeton University Press.

Varner, Gary. 1998. *In nature's interests? Interests, animal rights, and environmental ethics*. Oxford: Oxford University Press.

Von Wright, G. H. 1963. *The varieties of goodness*. London: Routledge.

Williams, Bernard. 1972. *Morality*. New York: Harper and Row.

———. 1976. Moral luck. Reprinted in *Moral luck*. Cambridge, United Kingdom: Cambridge University Press, 1981.

———. 1989. Internal reasons and the obscurity of blame. Reprinted in *Making sense of humanity.* Cambridge, United Kingdom: Cambridge University Press, 1995.

Wong, David. 1984. *Moral relativity.* Berkeley: University of California Press.

Ziff, Paul. 1960. *Semantic analysis.* Ithaca, New York: Cornell University Press.

Zimmerman, Michael J. 1999. In defense of the concept of intrinsic value. *The Canadian Journal of Philosophy* 29: 329–410.

Index

Abell, George, 22
abortion, 14, 16–17, 23, 26
absolutism, moral. *See* Moral Universalism, vs. Moral Relativism
action, 29
   kinds vs. classes, and defining Agent Relativism, 95–100
   paternalistic, 87
agent, 103n. 1
   fully informed, 39–48, 104n. 7
   fully rational (vs. irrational) 35, 40, 42, 45–46
Agent Relativism, xv, 6, 30, 103n. 3
   and consequentialism, 97–100
   and ought implies can, 33
Anscombe, G. E. M., 98–100
Appraiser Relativism, xiii, 3–4
   counterintuitive implications, 7–12
   and intractability of moral disagreement, xiii, xv, 6–7, 24–25
   outside of ethics, 91–93
   and reliability of linguistic intuitions, xiii–xiv, 23
Argument from the Best Explanation, xiii, 6–7
Argument from Extreme Heinousness, 31
Argument from Morally Relevant Differences, 31–32

Aristotle, 20–21
Armstrong, David, 108n. 3
astronomy, 20–21

Beardsley, Monroe, 85–86
belief ascriptions, moral, 10 – 12, 95
Bennett, Jonathan, 95–99
Bessel, Friedrich, 21
Best Explanation, Argument from, xiii, 6–7
Brahe, Tycho, 21
Brink, David, 35–36
Brower, Bruce W., 76–77

Carnap, Rudolf, 108n. 2
chastity, as an out-of-date aspect of morality, 65
cognitivism, cognitive (vs. noncognitivism), 5
   appraiser relativism, as a form of cognitivism, 5–6
comparison classes, 55, 60, 94
completing relatum, 17
consequentialism, and Agent Relativism, 97–100
consistency (inconsistency), of moral sentences, 8–9, 12–16, 102n. 7
context sensitivity, of moral sentences, 13
   and noncognitivism, 8

propositions as context independent entities, 101n. 1
  according to Salience Relativism, 11–12
  according to Speaker Relativism, 10–11
  truncated contexts, 12
contradiction, 3–4, 7
corpse, cadaver, 57, 61, 107n. 25

demonstratives. *See* context sensitivity, of moral sentences
desire, 104n. 7
  and correspondence to moral beliefs, 41
  and the Humean Theory of Motivation, 41
  as the source of reasons, 45–47
Desire Argument, 39–44
  Narrow, 44–47
  and motivation, 47–50
Dreier, James, 7–8, 101n. 2

egoism, ethical, 100
Einstein, Albert, theory of relativity, 16–18. *See also* Mass
Elder, Crawford, 60
Elizabeth, Queen, 74–75
evil, as something good in a way but not good simpliciter, 61
Explanation, 24–26

fact,
  (non) practical, defined, 44–45
  as reasons, 37
  See also Desire Argument, Narrow; Reasons for Action Thesis
Feinberg, Joel, 62–63
Feynman, Richard, 103n. 11
Foot, Philippa, 104n. 3, 106n. 20
forgery, 56–57, 60, 105n. 6

gavagai, 92–93
Geach, Peter, 55–57, 60

good, goodness
  as a determinable property, 60–61
  ethical, 84
  as an existential generalization, 59
  goodness-for, 61, 63
  as a property, 55, 58–59
  as source of reasons for action, 55
  varieties of, 58
  See also ways of being good
Goodman, Nelson, 108n. 2
Gowans, Christopher, xiv

Hare, R. M., 104n. 4
Harman, Gilbert
  on killing the innocent, 39, 41–43
  on Mass, 16–17, 101n. 3, 102n. 4
  on moral disagreements, 14–15, 22–23
  on Moral Relativism, 93–94
  on Motion, 18–19
  on naturalism and accounts of reasons for action, xvii, 45–50
  on ought implies can, 32
  on Salience Relativism, 11
harmless wrongdoing, 82
Heinousness, Argument from Extreme, 31
Hoskins, Michael, 21
human fulfillment, as defining a moral framework, 14

Imbornoni, Ann Marie, 105n. 6
immorality, immoralist, 4, 6, 8–11, 13, 35, 94, 107n. 23
incompleteness, of moral sentences, 17–18
inconsistency, in moral sentences, 8–12
  See also moral disagreement
indexical sentences, 8, 13
intent, of speaker vs. proposition asserted by a moral sentence, 5
interest
  function-based, 63

health-based, 63
  of plants, 62–63, 105n. 10
  reduced to wants, 62–63
  self, 37–38 (*see also* Egoism)
internalism. *See* Reasons Internalism;
  Moral Internalism
intrinsic properties, vs. relational properties, 85–86
intrinsic value, 84–87, 106n. 22
  as based on intrinsic properties,
    84–85
  vs. instrumentally good, 85–87
  of persons, 82, 84, 86–87
intuition
  brute vs. conclusion drawn from
    other beliefs, 42
  for the Practicality Requirement, 38
  pre-theoretical, 27
  See also linguistic intuitions

justice, just, (vs. injustice), 37–38,
  64–65, 71, 79, 82, 83

Kaplan, David, 102n. 6
killing the innocent, 39, 41–43,
  98–100
kind. *See* action, kind vs. classes
kindness, 76–77, 79, 89
Korsgaard, Christine, 37, 103n. 6

Lawrence, Gavin, 71–73
linguistic intuitions
  explaining away, 13–22
  about goodness, 55
  and logical relations of moral sentences, 3, 23, 93
  reliability of, 16–18, 23, 91, 108n.
    1
  and semantical rules, 91–93
  sensitivity to counterexamples, 15
Lyons, David, 5–6, 8, 103n. 2

Mackie, John, 49–50, 104n. 10
Mass, 16–17, 19, 22, 25

metaethical principle, general, 32
Moore, G. E., 55, 85
moral attitudes, 5, 102n. 7
moral belief ascriptions, 10–12, 95
moral disagreement, intractable
  as explained by appraiser relativism,
    6–7
  in fundamental moral issues, 26
  intuitions, about, 9, 13, 23–24,
    102n. 7
  range of, 14–15
  See also truth
Moral Internalism, 40–41
moral judgments. *See* propositions,
  moral
moral properties. *See* morality
moral qualities, relative to a moral
  framework, 16, 18, 23
Moral Relativism, 93–94
  and consequentialism, 97–100
  and deontology, 98–99
  and kinds of actions, 95–97
  and moral propositions, 94–95
  See also Moral Universalism
Moral Requirements Thesis, 66, 70
  argument for, 75–77
  See also ways of being good, morally
moral requirements, universal, 29
  reasons to comply with. *See*
    Practicality Requirement;
    Relevance of Morality
  relativity to circumstances, 31–32,
    95–97
  trivial vs. substantive, 96–100
moral sentences, 4–12, 23, 94, 102n.
  5
  completing relatum, 17, 103n. 11
  as incomplete, 17–18
  See also propositions, moral
moral status, as a basis for reasons for
  action, 107n. 22
moral system, of speaker, 14
Moral Universalism, 30
  arguments for, 31–32

and Desire Argument, 39, 42–44
  vs. Moral Relativism, 95–100
  and Reasons Internalism, 43
morality, 5, 23, 94
  as sets of propositions, 94–95
  salient to the speaker, 5
  of the speaker, 4–5
Morality, Authority of, 53
Morally Relevant Differences, Argument from, 31–32
Mother Teresa, 15, 23
Motion, 19–22, 25–26
motivation
  Humean Theory of, 40–41, 43, 48
  and reasons for action, xvi–xvii, 38, 47–50
  See also desire; Moral Internalism; Reasons Internalism
Murder Incorporated, 39

Nagel, Thomas, 46
necessarily (vs. contingently) normative, 78, 81–82, 87–88
Newton, Isaac, Newtonian physics, 7, 103n. 9
normative
  necessarily, 78, 81–82, 87–88
  facts. *See* fact, (non) practical, defined
numbers, matter morally, 31

ought implies can, 32
Overgeneralization, 13–14, 19, 22, 25

Plato, 37
Practicality Argument for Agent Relativism, 30, 33, 38, 51
Practicality Requirement, 30
  and Agent Relativism, 99–100
  defended, 35–38
  plausibility, 31
  and rational agent, 42
  and Reasons Internalism, 40–41
practical rationality
  formal object of, 72
  See also rationality, practical
promises, 32–33, 49, 97
propositions, moral, 8–9, 94–95, 101n. 1.
  See also morality, as sets of propositions
propositional attitudes, 10
Putnam, Hilary, 108n. 2

Quick Argument for the Relevance of Morality, 70, 75, 78, 88
Quine, Willard Van Orman, 91–93

rationality, 45
  agent. *See* agent, fully rational
  and being motivated by moral beliefs, 41
  and being motivated by normative beliefs, 40
  practical, 72–73
  See also Desire Argument; Narrow Desire Argument; reason for action
reason for action, 34–35
  agent-centered theory of, 45–48, 50
  desire-based theory of, 45–48, 50
  (virtue) good-based account of, 71–72
  good-for-the agent account of, 73–74
  having vs. existing, 34–35
  interest-based, 54
  naturalistic account of, 29, 38, 45–50
  non-moral, 36–37
  overriding, 34–36, 47, 53, 77.
  See also Reasons Internalism; Practicality Requirement
Reasons for Action Thesis, 66
  and ways of being good, 69
Reasons for Action Thesis, Revised, 69, 70
  advantages of, 73–74

problems with, 78–81
Reasons Internalism, 40, 42–43
   and Desire Argument, 39–41, 43
   Strong, 48–50
Reasons Relativism, 30–31, 51
   See also Desire Argument
Reese's Peanut Butter Cup, eating a, 59–60
relatum, completing, 17
Relevance of Morality, 53–54
   Quick Argument for, 70, 75, 78, 88
   Revised Argument for, 83
Ross, W. D., 56
Salience Relativism, 5
   counterintuitive implications of, 7–10, 11–12

Skepticism, skeptic, moral, 54, 89, 103n. 6
   practical vs. cognitive, 37
Smith, Michael, xvi
   See also Humean Theory of Motivation
Sobel, David, 103n. 5
speaker's intent, vs. proposition asserted by a moral sentence, 5
Speaker Relativism, 4–5
   counterintuitive implications of, 7–10, 10–11
Stevenson, Charles, 102n. 7
Strong Reasons Internalism, 48–50
Struve, Wilhelm, 21
subjectivism, 5
Superman, and Moral Universalism, 32–33
syntactic negation, 4, 6
   See also morality; moral sentences

Test, 17
   Mass, as potential counterexample to, 19
   mentioned, 23
   and semantic rules, 91–93

Thomson, Judith Jarvis
   on Salience Relativism, 11
   on virtue properties, 64–65, 106n. 13
   on ways of being good, xvii, 57–59, 63, 68, 107n. 24
Thrasymachus, 37–38
truncated contexts, 12
truth, truth ascriptions, 6–7, 12, 22–24
   and linguistic intuitions, 91–94

universal moral requirements. See moral requirements, universal

Varner, Gary, 105n. 10
Villain, 39–43, 99–100
virtue properties, virtuous, 64–65, 71, 106n. 15
Von Wright, G. H., 58

wants, 61–63
ways of being good (bad)
   aesthetical, 58
   for an Artifact Generalization, 78, 80–81, 82
   as basis of Relevance of Morality, 64
   commonness of meaning, 60
   and interests, 61–62
   morally, 64–65, 75–76
   possible misinterpretations, 58–60
   for a person, 78, 80, 82, 84
   and wants, 61–63
weakness of will, 46–47
   See also Reese's Peanut Butter Cup, eating a
Williams, Bernard, 35–36
Wong, David, 13–15, 17–18, 101n. 2
W2, and kindness as a way of being good, 76–77

Ziff, Paul, 57, 61, 107n. 25
Zimmerman, Michael J., 58, 84

For Product Safety Concerns and Information please contact our EU
representative GPSR@taylorandfrancis.com
Taylor & Francis Verlag GmbH, Kaufingerstraße 24, 80331 München, Germany

www.ingramcontent.com/pod-product-compliance
Lightning Source LLC
Chambersburg PA
CBHW052131300426
44116CB00010B/1861